Beautiful Hardship: My Story

B. Michael Fett

Millennial Mind Publishing
An imprint of American Book Publishing
5442 So. 900 East, #146
Salt Lake City, UT 84117-7204
www.american-book.com
Printed in the United States of America on acid-free paper.
Beautiful Hardship: My Story
Designed by Jana Rade, design@american-book.com

Publisher's Note: *American Book Publishing relies on the author's integrity of research and attribution; each statement has not been investigated to determine if it has been accurately made. The author and publisher specifically disclaim any responsibility for any liability, loss, or risk, personal or otherwise, which is incurred as a consequence, directly or indirectly, of the use and application of any of the contents of this book. In such situations where medical, legal, or other professional services may apply, please seek the advice of such professionals directly.*

Library of Congress Cataloging-in-Publication Data
Fett, B. Michael, 1967-
Beautiful hardship : my story / B. Michael Fett.
   p. cm.
Includes bibliographical references and index.
ISBN-13: 978-1-58982-555-0
ISBN-10: 1-58982-555-1
1. Fett, B. Michael, 1967- 2. Bodybuilders--United States--Biography. 3. Bodybuilders--Drug use. 4. Anabolic steroids. 5. Doping in sports. 6. Marines--United States--Biography. 7. United States. Marine Corps--Biography. 8. Air pilots--United States--Biography. I. Title.
CT275.F4855A3 2009
362.29092--dc22
[B]
                          2009011887

Special Sales

These books are available at special discounts for bulk purchases. Special editions, including personalized covers, excerpts of existing books, and corporate imprints, can be created in large quantities for special needs. For more information e-mail info@american-book.com.

Beautiful Hardship: My Story

B. Michael Fett

Dedication

To my mother for instilling within me the strength and determination it has taken me to get here.

Prologue

I was on my way to a part-time job in downtown Washington D.C. I stopped at McDonald's for a quick bite to eat. As I approached the door, I saw him. He was sitting on a piece of cardboard and positioned in the entrance to what was going to quell the stirring in my stomach. I continued on my path. He wasn't the first that I had encountered in this city. Washington D.C. is a magnet for the homeless.

My mind was two steps ahead savoring that sausage biscuit, but my eyes lost all concentration; they were staring at the bench man. He looked up and I could see that his eyes were empty. I was held captive to every feature of the bench man's face.

Reading the menu board, I continued to be preoccupied with the man sitting outside the door. I glanced at the window and I could see the top of his ragged, filthy hat bobbing every few seconds just above the windowsill.

"Give me two sausage biscuits, two hash browns, hot chocolate, and a coffee," I said, finally making a choice.

Bag in hand, I approached the door reluctantly. I had no idea how the Benchman would greet me when I offered him breakfast. I swung the door open. Benchman looked up, but he couldn't focus on me as the sun was shining in his eyes. I reached out, gripping the bag with two fingers and motioning it to him. I was juggling the hot cocoa and coffee in my other hand. He didn't move.

"I don't drink coffee, but it sure is burning my hand! I bought it for you. Besides, I'm half Jewish on my mother's side and if she finds out that I had to throw it away and waste that fifty cents, I'll be in trouble," I said.

Then I saw it; a smirk muscled its way into his face. Here was a man whose life had fallen on hard times, yet something inside of him made him acknowledge my attempt at humor. Without missing a beat, he uttered, "And what makes you think I want a burned hand?"

"Touché," I replied. "Well then I'll just have to deal with the wrath of a half Jewish woman." I plopped down on the cold concrete next to his cardboard sofa and began to eat my breakfast.

Benchman gazed at me in disbelief.

Benchman. It was such an impersonal title to have bestowed upon him. For all I knew, he could have been Socrates reincarnated. Why was I doing this? This was a moment that wouldn't be diminished by time or place or circumstance. I never asked Benchman for a name; never asked where he was from. I just waited for the story.

There's breakfast in that bag," I said. "And it won't burn your hand."

"Let me guess, if I don't eat it, your half Jewish mom is going to have a heart attack right?" he asked.

"No, but my Chinese father will probably Kung Fu me because I didn't bring him breakfast." The Berlin wall fell. His shoulders were shaking with laughter. He sensed that I was lying about my mother and of course I was.

We sat and ate our sausage biscuits in the cold brisk air. I could feel the heat from the steam vent we were sitting next to. He must have seen me looking at it.

"If you sit on top of it, your clothes will get soaked and you'll catch pneumonia, but if you sit over here, you won't get wet and you can still feel the warm air," he said. All this time, I thought he was there for the prospect of food. Shows you how much I knew about life as a benchman.

I wasn't sure how to ask my question or even if I should. You know the one, the one we all want to ask…how did you get here? What happened in life that brought you here? That's the beauty of the bench, you don't have to ask. It'll be forthcoming you just have to give it time. His story came in a few sentences here and a few ramblings there, and by reading between the lines I was able to piece it together. He lost his battle with the stock market in 1989; financial destitution. Those words had no meaning to me. They had no relevance. I grew up struggling in a single-parent home where paycheck to paycheck was all we knew. The very thought of stocks and bonds and mutual funds was way over my head, but I listened and I learned Benchman's personal plight.

The last words I got from Benchman? "You don't look Jewish, but tell your mom I drank the coffee!"

"Yeah I'm not, nor is she. Roman Catholic at heart she is. I just can't help, but think it would have been more fun to have a bar mitzvah than a confirmation," I replied.

He never said thanks. He didn't have to. I'm the one who should have said thanks. Our shared fifteen minutes wasn't about friendship or companionship. It wasn't about helping the homeless. I just wanted to know his story whether or not I could comprehend it with all its complexities was yet to be seen. The whole episode came and went. In fact, most of it didn't make sense until I found myself homeless. That's when the word destitute had meaning; that's when giving up on life became a reality.

This is the story of my journey on the road of life. It may be a bit inspirational for some; others may find it comical. What this story is; however, is true. It is my experience with a dark childhood followed by a successful launch into the sport of bodybuilding, culminating to a downward spiral into the black market of steroids. My story branches into the world of homelessness and financial ruin after the tragedy of September 11, 2001 and continues into the world of flying as a commercial pilot. This is how I corrected my mistakes and turned my life around for the better.

Table of Contents

CHAPTER 1

A Rocky Start

I entered this world in the tumultuous year of 1967. Vietnam was in full swing. President Johnson was increasing the troop count to continue his personal war against the North Vietnamese. A gallon of gas cost thirty three cents. An average new home cost fourteen thousand four hundred and twenty five dollars. Oh my! That was cheap even when the average income was only seven thousand three hundred dollars a year. There I was, the middle child of an eventual three.

My birthplace was Longmont, Colorado, but after my parents divorced, mom took the kids and relocated to Grandma's house in Iowa. I was four years old.

The town was Camanche and we stayed less than a year. Mom was very determined to make it on her own and at the first opportunity; she packed us up and moved to the neighboring town of Clinton.

At that time, Clinton was the place to be. Complete with a bustling downtown and a public bus system, it was an industrial town in full swing. Railroad yards and factories were running continuously with middle class folks who earned their keep by the time clock. These were the people that built this country; the guys pounding the steel in Pittsburgh, digging up the coal in West Virginia, and cranking out the corn byproducts in the factories of Iowa.

Clinton was a river town as well. The barges roared up and down the mighty Mississippi carrying cargo from Minnesota to New Orleans. It was a true "Tom Sawyer" playground. That river was the dirtiest, nastiest water known to man and I loved it. I loved everything about it. That river represented strength and tenacity and every once in a while it let the people along its shores know just how tenacious it could be. In the '70s, it reared its ugly head, all too often spilling over its banks into the heart of downtown.

If you've seen the film *A Christmas Story*, you can imagine Clinton, Iowa in the '70s. Downtown was unbelievably vibrant. Fifth Avenue at Christmas time was a sight to behold; the street's lamps covered with lights and decorations and snow.

I stood on one of the corners of Fifth Avenue in front of the YMCA, waiting in line to see Santa and I could feel the December air right down to my bones. Ah, but man it was worth it! Santa, you big fat liar in a red suit! It didn't matter. I was five and he was real. So what if I didn't get that pony or that machine gun the year before. I wasn't holding a grudge. Why should I? I had this plastic army paratrooper that he gave me. So, for the moment, my loftier wants would be put aside.

"Does this thing really work?" I asked. I launched the trooper into the air. It was immediately lost in the darkness. Then, poof, the chute opened! Slowly and methodically he fell, angelic like in his descent, dancing his way down crushing the snowflakes and impeding their own fall. It was magical. Right up to the moment where he landed in the hustle and bustle of Fifth Avenue. Suddenly, clinging to his rifle and helmet, my paratrooper was taken prisoner by the first vehicle that passed. Unable to free himself from what had blindsided him, the soldier's fate was out of my hands. My paratrooper had worked, but now he was helpless, clinging to the underside of a car while being dragged down the street.

Clinton, too, was blindsided when the factories moved outside the United States in search of cheaper labor. The railroads went bankrupt and the youthful workforce embraced computer technology, relocating to cities like Chicago and Milwaukee.

The retail in Clinton also vanished. Petersen's and Kline's fell in the wake of Wal-Mart. The old-fashioned movie theaters, complete with red velvet ropes and balconies, gave way to the Cineplex. The bus transit went south along with the population.

At that time, we were living at the Valley High Apartments. Mom was working at the nursing home and we had joined the world of welfare. At five, who cared? I had toys, I was going to school, and I had food and clothing. I had it all. I was the happiest kid in the world. I can't say the same for mom though. This was one of the most trying times of her life; single mom with three kids trying to make ends meet.

Valley High Apartments; I guess it was as good a place as any to start life over. We were a single-parent family trying to move up in life, but sometimes moving up isn't as easy as it sounds. Sometimes you have to experience something worse than what you have before you can truly move up. Our family had to do just that.

CHAPTER 2

Tom

His name was Tom. He had arrogance about him, but then all rebels of the '70s did. He wore his hair long around the shoulders and had a full beard. He rode a Harley and sported tattoos and was no stranger to the county lock up.

The apartment was too small for the five of us so we moved to a house on Fifth Avenue. It was four blocks from downtown and four blocks from the school. The house itself was a big 1930s concrete fortress. It had an attic that was as large as the main floor, but it was so dusty and dirty that we only used it for storage. The floor of the attic was made of hardwood and it creaked and moaned relentlessly. The basement was no better. It wasn't fit for a corpse. It was cold and damp down there, and the windows were clouded from age and grime. It harbored a dank, musty smell. There was space down there that was about six feet by three feet and it was all dirt. It was in the middle of the basement floor and had a concrete piece that was exactly like a tombstone at one end. It looked like a gravesite. I scared myself silly many times letting my imagination run with thoughts of what was down there.

The living area of the house was very out-of-date. The carpet had a 1930s flower design and it was a quarter-inch thick without padding. The room to the front of the house was separated by big wooden sliding doors that belonged in an old library or maybe in a mansion where the den was separated from another room. We never used the doors. Mom's room was connected to my sister's room with an adjoining closet. The hallway was large and the linen cabinets were built into the wall; all of them, old, shellacked and splintered wood. My brother and I shared a room at the back end of the house. It was a large room with hardwood floors.

The house was always cold. It had radiators that used hot water to heat the place. We had a back porch that was partially screened and covered with grapevines. The property had a garage as well, but it was in the same condition as the basement so we only used it to store bikes and tricycles.

It was a safe neighborhood with lots of kids. Making friends was easy and they all lived within walking distance. Hide and seek and flashlight tag became staple forms of entertainment among the kids.

At first, our life seemed normal. We did things as a family. We went camping and fishing and mushroom collecting. Tom loved the outdoors! I had no reason to suspect that anything was wrong until arguments between him and mom escalated into shouting matches and the shouting matches turned to fist fights. Mom no longer carried the smile that accentuated her high cheekbones. More often than not, she hid the results of Tom's temper behind her sunglasses.

I didn't understand him. He played the role of family man to a 'T' during the daylight hours, but after the sun went down, he won the Oscar for playing the demon seed. I can remember waking up one Saturday morning to watch cartoons only to find that he had thrown the TV at my mom the night before. It lay on the floor, shattered and covered with drywall pieces from the hole it had created when it hit the wall. No matter how violent he got, no matter how much pain he caused my mom, he always apologized the next day. After the TV incident, he bought her a vase full of roses, but when the sun went down, he threw the vase at her. I remember spending many nights huddled up with my dog trying to hide under my bed. Often times I would slip over to my sister's room and we would hide under the covers together.

I never talked about it to my friends. My neighborhood pal Gary had his own problems and in conversation with him one afternoon, he convinced me that we should run away. That was typical of a kid in second grade when he wasn't happy. Gary didn't know my reasons and I didn't know his, but we agreed it was the thing to do. That night I laid in bed till everyone went to sleep and in my house, that depended on how much Tom had to drink and when he was satisfied with how much he had abused my mother. This night it was around 11 o'clock. I packed a change of clothes, kissed my dog goodbye, and slipped out the back door. I crossed the street and ran down the alley to Gary's house.

"Gary? Are you there?" I asked into the darkness.

I waited and waited and waited. Gary had stood me up. I wandered back to my house and sat down under the street lamp hoping Gary would show. I waited till just before daybreak before going back inside. I didn't want to return.

Even at that age, I knew things weren't right in my world, but I didn't have the power to change them.

Life has defining moments, moments when you accept your consequences, moments when you change your ways, and moments that just define a point in time. For instance, if I were a professional football player, my defining moment might be my first touchdown. Not all defining moments are good however, and mine certainly was not. I awoke one night to my mother yelling, "Get off of me!" I knew it was going to be one of those nights. I could hear Tom laughing so I couldn't decipher between fighting and playing. Again I heard her voice and I slipped out into the doorway of the living room. Tom was on top of my mom; he had her hands pinned up behind her head. He was taunting her, laughing at her and hitting her as she moved her head from side to side to avoid the blows. I was as powerless as she was and I sulked back to my room. My mom's fate was out of my control. To this day, that image burns inside of me. I have never felt that helpless in all my life. I lay in my bed that night and cried myself to sleep.

I led a sort of double life while Tom lived with us. I would put on the smiley face at school and be on my best behavior at Grandma's house. Don't tell Grandma this and don't say anything about that. I did it all. I did it out of love for my mom. My siblings and I were running a smoke screen for her, but in the end, all of our lies and all of our tactics of deception couldn't hide the black eyes and the bruises.

How much is enough? I'm not sure when my mom decided that she wasn't going to stand for it anymore. I'm truly amazed that after being treated so badly by Tom, she was able to find her way back to self worth. I think she just kept telling herself that things would get better and they eventually did. It was the day she left him, head held high and pride leading the way. I remember the night before it happened, the shouting and screaming, the precursor to Tom's wrath. The hatred swelled inside my chest and choked me to sleep.

That morning I tiptoed out to see the aftermath. Would it be the TV? Would it be broken dishes or pictures? I spotted the first sign of the battle. The phone cord had been yanked out of the wall and the phone lay on the floor with the receiver stretched to its cord length. I wondered if mom had tried to call for help. Before I could continue my reconnaissance, mom came from the hallway behind me.

"Go get dressed, we're going to Grandma's," she said.

I turned to see her, her face swollen. Her eyes told the story of the night before only this time they said something more; they said, "I've had enough." She was headed to my sister's room. I went back to my room to find my brother getting dressed.

Mom loaded us into the car and I waited for the instructions of what I shouldn't say at Grandma's house, but the instructions never came. The words I remember were, "We're going to go live with Grandma for a while." I looked at the determined woman who had had her fill of what life was throwing her way and I pictured her, head held high, makeup flawlessly accentuating the features of her face, and her hair blowing in the wind. I pictured it, but today wasn't the day it was going to happen. Scars don't heal so quickly. But for all that *wasn't* going to happen that day, something did; a new lease on life, a second shot at redemption, a new and better life for a woman and her kids. It was out there somewhere and my mom was determined to find it.

CHAPTER 3

Life After Tom

After Tom, we landed at Grandma's house for a while. She had moved into a house that was a little more adapted to accommodate the traveling circus that we had become. And besides, anything was better than what we had left behind.

I don't quite understand how the thought process works for parents when they encounter important decisions regarding their children. My understanding now is about the same as it was then, when my third year of elementary school resulted in an abrupt adieu to the public school system and an enrollment in Clinton's Sacred Heart Catholic School. I have never understood the purpose of a religious anything; let alone forcing your child to incorporate a belief in God with his ABC's. Religious schooling…take money from the lying faction called government and give it to the tax evasion coalition called 'The Church' for the purpose of educating children in the false hope that they will get a better and somewhat higher sense of learning. I didn't buy into it then and I don't buy into it now. My mom, however, bought it hook, line, and sinker.

At the start of my third grade year, we hadn't made our move from the house on Fifth Avenue. We were still six months away from leaving. I was reluctant to go to school on that first day. New kids and new surroundings were a little daunting to say the least and on top of that, I was carrying the baggage of a home life that was more than a little bit off kilter. I never understood why schools insist on keeping new students in the office before sending them off to class. It only makes the grand entrance into the classroom a bit more traumatic if, for instance, you drop your books upon entering the room. So was the case with me. I spilled my books on the floor as I walked in during roll call. The laughter commenced, subsided and commenced again when the teacher called my name.

It didn't take long to fit in with this group. Most didn't survive the Catholic school system any longer than I did. Some had secrets like mine, which gave me the comfort of a common bond and like me; they were eventually reclaimed by the public school system to receive the exact same education that their parents had hoped enrollment in Catholic school would bring.

I was hoping that after our move to Camanche, the great distance from Sacred Heart would severely strain my ability to keep perfect attendance. No such luck. Even while we were holed up at Grandma's in Camanche, that school bus managed to find me. Grandma's house butted up against an open field that separated the dwelling from the Central Steel Tubing Company. In the middle of that field lay dirt trails that most of the kids used to ride their bicycles and motorcycles on. Today, however, marked the first time that a school bus driver from Sacred Heart would use those trails to locate two eventual commuters. The feeling of humiliation came over my brother and me as we watched the bus struggle through the trail overran with tall brush and laden with potholes. The bus bounced and rocked its way through the field finally coming to a halt outside our front door. The other kids would never let us live it down. Staying at Grandma's was only a temporary fix, however, and we soon found ourselves back in Clinton.

We were now living in a low cost apartment complex on the north end of town. The apartments were converted from a former women's reformatory and at that time only a few of the buildings had been renovated. The complex was called The Village and it was located on Clinton's north side tucked away from everything. There were no playgrounds or kids to make friends with. Mom was doing what she had to do to make ends meet and that meant working constantly. I recall many babysitters, but most of the time it was one of my two aunts.

The layout of the apartment was ridiculous. The living room was connected to a small kitchen and both were connected to a hallway that was a five-dollar cab ride away from the bedrooms and the bathroom.

Defining moments of our time here? There are two: The first of which involved my brother and that lengthy hallway. Every now and then this story surfaces at a family gathering and I can't help, but laugh. It involved my brother's stubborn will to not clean the bathroom versus my aunt's overbearing technique to see that the chore was done.

"Get in there and clean that up!" was the command. The response we all heard was "No." I don't know why he said it.

I can only imagine it was a fourth grader's momentary lapse of reason that forced him to spit those words out.

"What did you say?" she asked. Here was his chance at redemption. Certainly he would realize his faux pas and correct himself. Then, as if the apparently brain damaged child couldn't fathom the seriousness of the situation, he again replied, "No." I looked at my aunt, she looked at me and without batting an eye she again turned her sights to the one who would not conform.

By the time my brother came to the realization that the bathroom would be cleaned voluntarily or otherwise, it was too late. She picked him off the floor by his leg and began dragging him in the direction of the bathroom that made its home three-quarters of a mile away. If only she had the strength to continue her hold on him, he would have had, at the very least, a free ride to the end of the hallway, but she didn't and so he didn't. She tired, but not to the point where she wasn't able to throw him the final stretch of the hall. I'm sure he cursed that hallway for being so long. His ordeal didn't stop until the hallway ended. I could have intervened. I could have cleaned the bathroom, but this was more than a beating bestowed upon a child who had no respect for rules and discipline, it was payback by proxy. It was the revenge that I couldn't give, for every fight that I had lost to him, for every toy of mine that he had broken; the beating was justified. He had two chances to steer the course of his fate. Such a pity he fell short by one letter in giving the correct response. 'No!' turns to "Now?" so easily. When it was over, I offered nothing more than false moral support.

The next defining moment of our stay at The Village happened while I was at school. I was at recess when the fire station bell went off. The station sat on the corner opposite the school building. We saw the trucks roll out onto the road and head north. We all cheered and waved as they swung around the corner, the men with their coats half buttoned, holding onto the chrome rail at the tail of the vehicle.

Fire trucks and sirens are nothing more than mild interruptions of daily traffic flow or distractions to the midday daydream. When you're a victim, however, it takes on a whole new meaning. My brother and I stepped off the school bus that afternoon to find part of our house lying in the courtyard between the apartment buildings. There was no mistake that the contents belonged to us. We entered the building with our heads hanging. Why us? Hadn't we suffered enough already? The apartment was still reeking and smoke was still hanging about. Scorching burn marks lined the walls and ceiling of my sister's bedroom. Once again we heard those familiar words, "We're going to go stay at Grandma's."

CHAPTER 4

Camanche, Iowa

The 'e' is silent, which always confused me since our school mascot was a Comanche Indian. The town itself was located on the shores of the mighty Mississippi pushed as far east as the Iowa state line would allow. It's a little river town complete with a bank, a post office, a barbershop, and a mom-and-pop grocery store. At one time, it even had a fully operational traffic light. It was Mayberry.

The population was comprised of middle class laborers. Some of the town's families were more traditional with two and a half kids and a white picket fence, and some were having their day-to-day struggles with life on the farm, but all were Midwesterners; easy going folk that would help you with a flat tire or push you out of a snow bank. They were people with morals and ethics and a general desire to help. They drank pop and they ate supper and they liked their beer on Friday night. The neighborhoods were safe and the schools were the best in the state.

By this time, Mom had left the nursing home and said good-bye to the bartending job that followed it. She landed a job with the rest of the middle class strugglers in Camanche. She traded the shot glass for the time clock at one of the local factories and bought a little house on Sixteenth Avenue.

The school was a ten-minute walk. Every kid in town walked to school. It didn't matter where you lived; it was close enough to walk. If you rode the bus, it was a sure sign that you lived in the country. That was the good thing about a small town; you never heard the old adage, "you can't get there from here," because nothing was ever really far away.

The neighborhood was full of kids. I had a friend in every other house. We played baseball in the fields behind the houses and football in the backyards. We built tree houses and caught snakes and turtles. We had fistfights on occasion and we played hide and seek and flashlight tag as well.

I know mom saw Tom on occasion, but deep down she knew he would never change. She had her pride now and the self-determination to move on. I never saw Tom at our house in Camanche, but that didn't mean I wouldn't see him again.

The summer before fourth grade was like all the summers of my childhood. I got up early and ran outside to see who was already out there and what they were doing. I could see the house across the street that lay tucked behind the corner house. That's where my buddy Leon Kendall Walton, a.k.a. Kendall, lived. His mom called him Kendall because his dad was Leon Sr. It was something that only the neighborhood knew. He was Leon at school, but that didn't stop the neighborhood kids from doing their best imitation of his mother on school grounds with a heart stopping thunderous yell. "Kendall!" We did it just to see him jump at the thought that his mother was there and he was in trouble.

It was 8:00 a.m. and I was looking for signs of life in the direction of his house. Parents were nowhere to be found. They were all grinding it out in the work-a-day world or they were still sleeping trying to recover from the brutal shift work that so many of them did. Kendall's parents were working. We didn't know the meaning of the word babysitter in the daylight hours of those summers in Camanche.

Get out of bed man! I thought. *There's so much to do! We're wasting the day away!* My insides turned with every movement of the second hand on our kitchen clock. 8:02 a.m. *I can't take it anymore.* I picked up the phone and made the call. No one answered. *That's it; I'm going over there. I'll make just enough noise outside of his house that he'll have to wake up! I can't believe he hasn't called yet!*

"Kendall!" I hollered at the front of the house. It was my best attempt at being subtle. Suddenly, there was life. The window slowly opened. It was his sister. She peeked out through the dirty screen.

"I'll get him," she said. 8:06 a.m., the front door cracked open. It was Kendall, eyes wide shut.

"Are you coming out?" I asked.

"I can't, I have to do my chores," he replied. *Chores? You must be kidding.*

"Do you want me to help you?" I asked.

"Ok," he replied. I slipped through the crack of the door and witnessed the list of chores that his mom had left him. It was the exact list that my mom had left me. Do the dishes, take out the trash, sweep the floor… It was basic sweatshop child labor abuse, but it was doable.

"You go get dressed and I'll start on this!" I commanded. I grabbed the broom in one hand and the dishtowel in the other. I had the dustpan pinched between my toes and both of my hands were moving hastily in all directions! The dishes were dried almost as soon as they left the rinse cycle. I was a machine on a mission! We had things to do. 8:15 a.m., I stumbled out of the kitchen. The sparkle was blinding. I was convinced it was the cleanest kitchen on the planet. It made me feel guilty for the mediocre performance that I displayed in cleaning my own kitchen, but not so much that I was going to do it again mind you. Parents don't really expect you to give your all in such a situation, do they? I heard the floor creak. It was Kendall. He had one sock on with his belt hanging out of the loop undone. He was foaming at the mouth with toothpaste. He sat down on the top step of the split-level home and put his shoes on. His timing was impeccable. Leon Kendall Walton Jr., the flim-flam man. He could have sold me a swamp in Florida that morning. He did this to me all the time. If his mother only knew it was me who cleaned her house during the summer! 8:30 a.m. We mounted our bikes. Out into the street we rode with the wind rushing passed our ears.

"So what do you want to do?" I asked.

"I don't know," he replied. "Do you think Bill's awake?"

By the time school started in August, I already had friends. Fourth grade was much less intimidating that way. I was finally feeling like a normal kid. I walked to school like a normal kid with books tucked up under my arm. On occasion, I got beat up by an older bully the same as the other kids. It was all normal. Mom was punching the time clock at twelve-hour intervals, just like everybody else. I no longer had to keep secrets stemming from what went on at home and the feeling was intoxicating. From the view out of my tiny bedroom in that little house, things were looking pretty good.

Fourth grade turned to fifth and our family blended in with the rest of them. I know that mom struggled to make ends meet, but as kids we never knew we were poor. We had shoes, clothes, bikes, fishing poles, and when it came time to play with the other kids; we had bats, balls, and gloves just like they did. The kids I hung out with were just like me. We all had that special lunch meal ticket at school that said "you'd have to get robbed to get any poorer" and we didn't care. We all wore our brother's hand me downs and we didn't care.

It was about this time Mom met and eventually married Steve. I liked him right from the start. He entered my life at a time when a boy needs a father figure. He had some resemblance to Tom in his physical attributes. He wore a mustache, had hair to his shoulders and he had a Harley, but that's where the similarities ended. Steve had a good job and he cared; not just about my mom, but about all of us. He had three children from a previous marriage so this wasn't his first go at being a father. I vividly recall a time when I was angry about something, and though I don't remember the exact reason, I do remember how Steve handled it. He sat right next to me on the edge of my bed and said, "I know I'm not your dad. I don't want to be your dad. I want to be your friend." That's how he started his speech and it struck a chord with me. This man had just gained all my respect and friends we became.

It was about this time that I took a tremendous focus on the sport of bodybuilding. Steve personally built me a mini gym in the corner of our basement. He also played a role in sparking my interest in flying. Whether it was mom, Steve, or my grandfather's doing, I received my first airplane ride in sixth grade when I flew from Chicago to Buffalo with him and grandpa on a business trip. I knew right then and there that I wanted flying to be a part of my life; I just didn't know how to make it happen.

With Steve around, we had a family unit. We ate supper between 5 and 6 p.m. just like everybody else. We even had a vacation at Disneyland. He brought stability to our home. I was the luckiest kid in the world. Then, it happened; that defining moment. It was late at night. The phone rang. *Who would call here at this time of night?* I asked myself. Mom had strict rules about phone usage after nine p.m. Don't do it or else! That was the rule. A second ring. *What if it's for me?* I thought, fearful of the repercussions. I couldn't take the chance. I had fallen asleep downstairs watching TV that night, which put me in close proximity to one of the phone extensions. I grabbed the receiver at the very exact moment that my mom picked up on the extension upstairs. She didn't know I was on the phone. It was Steve; he was in Europe on business.

The conversation started off with idle chitchat, but found its way to the center of what they really wanted to talk about. They talked about Steve's infidelity. Only a sixth grade education, but my brain was holding up the "uh oh" sign. I had no clue. Mom had known, but she wore the game face like a pro. I thought everything was golden in our world. Don't stare at the sky too long because the earth beneath you is still moving! They continued to talk and the conversation steered its way to divorce. Tears rolled down my cheeks. I knew the man that I loved so dearly was going to be leaving. Mom asked him if he would still come by the house and visit because, "Bret really thinks the world of you." He said he would. He promised, but it was all a lie. The only sound in the basement was my heart being ripped out and discarded so dispassionately.

The next time I saw Steve, he was packing all of his belongings. The three of us kids were sitting in the kitchen waiting for the inevitable. He walked passed us headed for the door, stopped, turned and said, "See you guys." That's it? You've got to be kidding me! He was out the door for less than two minutes when he burst back in, tears flowing down his cheeks. He grabbed all three of us and in a broken voice he said, "It just isn't that easy." We hugged for what seemed like an eternity. I didn't want to let him go. I knew that when I did, he would be gone forever, a fate that I wasn't ready to accept.

I never saw Steve again. I always wondered what happened to him. I wanted the opportunity to regale him with stories of my bodybuilding success and to see the approval on his face upon hearing that I was a commercial pilot. I thought he would have loved to hear those things. When mom called a few years back to tell me that he had passed way, my heart broke again for a man who I loved so dearly.

Life became very lonely after Steve left. Mom was working a lot and my brother and I were getting into school sports. We were a family unit that worked independently. Is that possible? We didn't have family sit down meals anymore. All of us kids could cook, clean, and do laundry. We didn't need a babysitter so the feeling of independence was ramped. We existed, but we didn't bond. I believe my sister and my mom were the closest out of the four of us.

The Christmas after Steve departed really reinforced the feeling of being in a non-traditional family. We opened our presents on Christmas Eve before mom went to work the graveyard shift. She had outdone herself this year. We got everything we asked for. Our lists had not gone unnoticed. Mom was watching, making sure we were happy, desperately hoping to have gotten Christmas right. I could see that she wasn't happy though and the reasons weren't all too clear.

Somewhere in the world Cinderella was losing a slipper; the clock struck midnight and mom had since left for work. I looked around the basement and tried to fathom the amount of money she had spent to see that we had a good Christmas. What is a good Christmas anyway? Is there such a thing as a bad one? Materialistically, it was a great Christmas, but emotionally it wasn't. My siblings were asleep, mom was punching the time clock and I was cleaning up wrapping paper and pine needles. The house had never seemed so empty before.

Aside from the things that were or were not going on at home, seventh grade was an exhilarating experience; junior high school. We were moving up in the world and we didn't have to walk as far on those cold January days since the school was a half-mile closer to the house than the Elementary School.

On the first day of junior high, I met my soon-to-be best friend, Jeffrey Lee Fall. Jeff had a seat in the front, facing the class; the teacher had him isolated from everybody else, because she knew what kind of kid Jeff was. This wasn't her first go around with Mr. Fall. She was writing the word "detention" on the chalkboard and explaining to the new student faculty the offenses for which one could have his or her name added to the column. Mr. Fall, who had been gracefully reclining in his chair, balancing on two legs with his arms crossed in a pose of perfect adolescent arrogance, fell backwards and smacked his head. He did what anyone would have: He blurted out the first obscenity that came to mind.

Without so much as batting an eye, the teacher walked over and awarded Jeff the coveted honor of being the first to have detention. I looked around the room at my buddies. We all smiled and the general consensus was that this kid was going to be our friend.

Seventh grade was the foundation for my juvenile delinquency. It started off with small pranks like shooting paper clips from rubber bands, and dumping someone's glue in art class to more elevated stupidity that involved hot wiring mopeds and drugs and alcohol. That's what junior high was; it was a learning experience that had nothing to do with book smarts. It was a place to build a reputation before passing through the doors of high school. Jeff Fall's reputation was already solidified on the first day of school. It didn't take long for the rest of us to follow his lead. Out of the 280 some odd days that are in a given school year, I probably spent 200 of them on that same detention list. I made an appearance in the principal's office more often than I could count. I had my share of fights in the futile attempt to build my own reputation, but no matter what I did or how hard I tried, I would never be able to topple the bad boy persona that Jeff rendered. He was the king. When Jeff said "lets hot wire that kid's moped and go for a ride," we all said, "you can't do it," but after his lunchtime joy ride through town had terminated, he gloated, smiling from ear to ear in the backseat of a police car. He had proved everybody wrong. The behavior seemed extreme if all he wanted was a half-day off from school.

All Jeff needed was a 10% chance of success and it was a go. Vegas odds aren't in a person's favor unless there's a better than 75% chance of winning. Jeff always sided with the underdog. If you said "Jeff you can't do that," he would prove you wrong.

Jeff and I became best friends. We walked to school together often, but that all depended on which days Jeff decided to go to school. He hated school and struggled through it. He had a reputation for skipping and I must admit I was right there with him on many occasions. Not because I hated it and certainly not because I was struggling with it. My reasons were simple, I wanted to do something different and Jeff never failed to provide a worthwhile itinerary.

The day Jeff and I planned our most defiant Houdini act from Camanche Junior High School was completely spur of the moment. It was 7:00 a.m., the sky was overcast and I was headed downstairs to start my day with a hot shower. The basement was always numbing in winter and the utility room had no carpet to buffer the cold from the concrete floor as it made its way into the soles of your feet. The bathroom was tiny. The door had to be closed to get around the toilet and step into the shower, but it wouldn't close tightly due to faulty construction so no matter how hot the shower got, you always knew that the chilling cold air of winter was waiting for you when you stepped out. The showers never lasted long in my house. Three kids all trying to get to school at the same time and all three needing showers. The last person always suffered and on this day, I was the last one.

I was turning the water knobs in every hot-cold combination in search of lukewarm. It would have satisfied my desire at that moment. Nothing. The cold knob was full left and the hot full right. I stared at the tiny streams of water, begging, pleading for enough hot water to wash my hair.

I hollered at my brother as the door upstairs slammed. He was out the door before I could voice my anger for the lack of hot water. He did this on purpose. He probably didn't even shower. I was willing to bet that he stood there with the hot water running, waving his hand through the falling stream, waiting for the hot to dissipate. It was cold and calculated and there's no doubt in my mind that I would have done the same to him.

"Ring" I rushed to the phone. I never understood the practice of waiting for the second ring. It seemed so trivial. If you pick it up and no one is there, hang up. My mom was famous for that maneuver always waiting for the second ring to justify expending the energy of retrieving the receiver.

"Hello," I answered.

"What are you doing?" Jeff asked.

"Trying to take a shower, but there's no hot water," I replied.

"You can shower over here," he said.

"That's ok, I'll just eat first," I replied.

"I'm not going to school today," he stated as a matter of fact.

"What are you going to do?" I asked.

"I'm thinking about taking my dad's snowmobile out," he replied. "Do you want to go? He won't be home until 4." It was a question followed by an affirmation that we wouldn't get caught. Jeff Fall already had the 10% chance of getting away with this act weighed out.

"I'll be over," I said. I went back to my room and stuffed my books under my bed. I sniffed under my arms and came to the conclusion that I didn't really need that shower. Good enough for me!

I trudged through the snow to Jeff's house. The snow was falling from the overcast above and the wind was still. So still that it made me want to stop walking just to see if I could hear the snowflakes hit the ground. The cold, however, made me quicken my pace.

I arrived at his house and banged on the door. He answered with a bit of irritation in his voice.

"What did you knock for?" he asked. Jeff never knocked at anyone's house. He generally cracked the door and announced that he was there. Drove my mom nuts! "Doesn't he know how to knock?" she would ask. I would look at her bewildered, shrug my shoulders and reply, "Mom, it's Jeff."

"We have to pull it out," he said. "I checked the gas already; it's full, so as long as we fill it up, my dad won't know," he continued. He handed me his snowmobile suit. "Here, you wear this one; I'll wear my dad's because it's going to be cold."

I was struggling with the snowmobile suit. It was too big and had too many zippers. The shoulder straps weren't adjusted right and I expressed my complaint verbally.

"Do you want to go or not?" he asked. I shut my mouth and followed him out the door stumbling in the suit.

The shed where his dad kept the snowmobile was an old rust bucket, but it served its purpose of providing shelter for the snowmobile and the lawnmower. Jeff was clearing a path through the deep snow and wrestling with the shed doors.

"Grab this thing," he commanded. We huffed and grunted, falling down more than once in our attempts to free the sled from the bonds of the shed. In fact, after we had the snowmobile out, we had to sit and rest to catch our breath. He checked the oil and gas again as if he had doubts with his previous findings. He turned the key and started it on the first try. "Meet me out front!" he hollered over the roar of the engine. I turned in the direction of the front yard and I heard Jeff rev the engine. My heart was pumping; this was going to be a day to remember.

He came around the corner and motioned me onto the back of the seat. I jumped on and grabbed hold of the sides. Jeff lifted his windscreen, turned to me and hollered, "You ready?" I gave him thumbs up and he gave it full throttle. I hadn't had enough time to reset my grip on the seat and as the snowmobile lunged forward, I went reeling in the opposite direction. Jeff looked back. He quickly let loose of the throttle. I rolled over to one side and picked myself up. Jeff lifted his helmet windscreen. He had tears in his eyes from laughing so hard. When he was finally able to speak, he told me to "hang on this time, dummy!"

I remounted and wrapped my arms around Jeff's rib cage. I shrunk down and drove my helmet into the middle of his back. Jeff sunk so his helmet was even with the windshield. He revved the engine as if to warn me and then he once again gave it full throttle. The tracks bit into the snow with the power of a team of horses, she ate the empty space that lay out in front of us. I could feel myself slipping to the back of the seat, but I had the death grip on Jeff. If I was going to fall off again, he was coming with me!

We approached the main road and Jeff's helmet moved left then right, he eased off the accelerator, but only long enough to bolster his confidence that he could take the turn at a fast clip. We rolled out of the turn and the houses went by in a blur. This hunk of metal had more power than anything I had ever experienced.

Jeff turned us onto what is now a four-lane highway that circumvents the thriving metropolis of Camanche. How could anyone not want to drive through our sleepy little town? Back then the highway project had been started and then stopped due to problems with the funding; however, the dirt was laid and leveled and it went on for miles. We had the perfect snowmobile trail. Jeff brought the machine to a halt. I peeked around his shoulders and my heart started pounding for there was nothing out in front of us except a sea of white and a ten-mile stretch of trail. He revved the engine; that was my cue. I reaffirmed the death grip as the Yamaha begged to be let loose. Jeff granted its wish. The speedometer buried beyond 90 mph, I leaned back and screamed at the top of my lungs, "Faster baby faster!" Jeff took one hand off the wheel and leaned back with me. We howled in unison as Jeff pumped his fist in the air.

A ten-mile stretch couldn't hold two teenagers captive for long and on our second run we spotted something or rather someone that Jeff was all too familiar with, and that was the town police officer. Though Camanche had three at that time, this one was the only one we ever crossed paths with. Affectionately known as Pizza Face for the scars left by childhood acne, the town cop stood next to his squad car parked at our original starting point. Jeff slowed down so he could focus on what lay ahead and after positive identification of the man in blue, Jeff turned to me, lifted his windscreen and said those all too familiar words, "Watch this!"

I had no choice, but to go along. I was a prisoner hanging on for dear life. The metal bullet lunged into the last quarter mile between us and Pizza Face. We were gaining ground at an alarming rate, but Jeff knew what he was doing. He was calculated and precise and when he slammed on the brake, we skidded to one side. He was more than prepared and yanked the wheel in the opposite direction so that we were moving sideways. He got the machine back in line with our backs pointed at the long arm of the law. We were within fifteen feet of Pizza Face and kicking up snow in his direction. Jeff fed it more gas and the speeding bullet gobbled up the blank space in the opposite direction. Thankfully, both of our helmets had visors and he had no idea who we were.

"We're going to the river," he cried out. Five miles down the trail we left its open space and made our way to the frozen waters of the Wapsipinicon River (a.k.a. the Wapsi).

Once off the beaten path, we joined the trails that led us into the woods surrounding the river. The trails were well traveled and Jeff knew most of them. The roar of the snowmobile was the only sound to break the peace and quiet of the wilderness that lay buried beneath the snow.

The snowmobile rode over the landscape, traveling sometimes at unrelenting speeds and other times at a crawling pace. She was a wonderful tour guide, but for all of her outstanding abilities, her sense of direction was lacking. She relied on Jeff's ability to navigate and Jeff relied on me to confirm his somewhat lacking knowledge of the terrain. For all of our efforts, the inevitable happened and we found ourselves lost. Ducking in and out of the forest and riding atop the frozen waters of the Wapsi, we passed a sign that said "Wildlife Refuge" more than once in our efforts to find the correct course. Jeff stopped the machine when we exited the trees for a third time. Nothing was familiar. The Wapsi might as well have been the Mississippi; it all looked the same. He walked out onto the ice looking in all directions to convince himself that he knew where we were.

"There it is!" he exclaimed. I walked out to where he was, but he was already climbing back on the machine. "There's what?" I asked myself.

We headed back the way we came. The "Wildlife Refuge" sign passed by in a blur. Jeff had found the trail that he was looking for and turned for it. If nothing else, it was a new course, which bolstered my confidence that we were headed in the right direction. The trail led us back into the trees and our pace slowed. It brought us face to face with an inlet stream that carried water from the Wapsi. Snowmobile tracks had already scarred the ice of the inlet, but Jeff spotted the watery glisten that the sun, peeking through the treetops, was able to expose. He stopped the sled in its tracks.

"What do you think?" he asked. We were both convinced that this was the way. Jeff walked out onto the ice. A calm feeling washed over me. This was the way, I was certain.

I didn't answer and with that we rode out onto the frozen stream. The watery layer covering the ice was deeper than we both had realized, indicative of the warmer than normal temps for that time of year. The Yamaha tiptoed across the twenty-five-foot span of ice. Jeff gunned the accelerator looking over his shoulder to see the water spray behind us. For all the power that the snowmobile had, when given the throttle in this manner, she wouldn't budge. Jeff continued to spray water and began to rev the engine; fast then slow, fast then slow, both of us laughing and admiring the distance the water traveled from underneath us.

The water show was captivating to say the least. With our attention diverted, the machine saw this as an opportunity to relax and catch her breath. And relax she did, so much that the rear of the snowmobile began to sink. The water began to rise on our tail. Jeff panicked and gave it full throttle. We lunged across the last five feet of the inlet gripping water and soft ice. I was caught off guard, I grabbed Jeff's coat and in doing so, caught him off guard and forced him to pull back on the handlebars. The machine interpreted this as a command to fly and fly she did. The nose was now pointed to the sky as she caught the embankment. Her tracks bit into the packed snow and launched us into the air. I fell backwards landing half in and half out of the partially frozen stream. Jeff tumbled off right after me. The snowmobile climbed up a tree as if she had claws and hung there suspended above Jeff.

I was speechless and terrified that it would fall down on top of us. Simultaneously we rolled out of the way. Jeff pulled himself to his feet and dusted off his pride. Neither one of us had a clue how to release a hunk of metal this size from the grips of the tree, but we knew we had to figure it out quickly or it would be the end of us!

The snowmobile hung there lifeless. Jeff surveyed it from every angle trying to decipher the best way to dislodge it. We agreed that the only way we would be able to remove it from the limbs would be sheer strength and brute force and at fourteen, we had neither. That notwithstanding, we tugged on the rear end, but the branches refused to let go. We had to stop at least once to catch our breath. The battle waged, but in the end, the tree was defeated and the snowmobile came crashing down. Not a dent; not a scratch. We removed the limbs from the front skis, then, the laughter broke out. Jeff pointed at me and made fun of the fact that I was wet from the knees down. We saddled up once again. Jeff wiped away tears from laughing and I shook the water off my lower extremities. After a few tries, the machine came to life.

Jeff was confident in the direction he was taking us. We didn't realize how far from home we were until we reached the town of Princeton. At that point, we were familiar enough with our surroundings to know that we were thirty minutes from home. The laughter commenced again and continued right up to the point when the engine quit. Had it happened ten minutes prior, we would have been in a pickle, but as it was, the gas station was thirty yards in front of us. Even though it was a bit of bad luck, it went unnoticed. Between us, we were able to scrounge three dollars, which was three more than we normally had and just enough to get us back to Jeff's house. No, we didn't get away with the perfect crime. Fresh snowmobile tracks in the yard and a warm engine made sure of that, but that was just part of being young and dumb.

Junior high continued to be a prankster's playground. We made teachers cry. We vandalized and we shoplifted. I gave up scholastic sports in eighth grade. The way I saw it, there was no sense in dragging out the inevitable. I was too short to play basketball, too slow to run track and too small to play football. Baseball was and still is too boring to hold my attention.

As we all know, the older you get, the more money you need and at age fourteen going on fifteen, I was finding myself in that very situation. I had a moped that needed gas and I was now a member of a local gym with monthly dues. I had no idea where to look for work and no clue of what I could do. That's how I ended up at the auto body shop where Tom worked. It had been a few years since I had last seen him. Those years hadn't been kind to him. It was obvious that he had been doing a lot of drinking and drugs. I stood in the doorway to the shop. Tom looked up from his sander and removed his goggles. He just stared. It wasn't a happy reunion. I was tucking my tail between my legs and asking for help from a man that I loathed. Words didn't come easy for either of us. He walked over to me and I could see the guilt plastered on his face. He wanted to apologize for all the hurt he had caused. I could feel it. He acted like a man who was ready to take his punishment when he stated, "You're either here to knock the daylights out of me or you're looking for work." Oh I desperately wanted to hit this man. The horrific scenes from the Fifth Avenue house came crashing down on me at that moment. I thought of all the pain my mom had endured because of him and I balled my hands into fists. I must have reeked of hatred at that moment.

"Well, which is it?" he asked.

"I'm looking for work," I said stuffing my hands in my pockets.

"I need someone to clean the shop," he offered.

"I can do that," I replied.

He pointed to the broom and gave me some instruction as to what needed to be done. It was usually a short day and a quick twenty bucks. On more than one occasion, I ended up tracking him to his watering hole to get my money. It was rather sad to see him this way. I showed up at 8:00 a.m. and he was at the bar by eleven.

I almost got that apology from him one Saturday after I finished cleaning. I tracked him to the bar and he put his arm around me and introduced me to his friends. He introduced me as if he were a proud father. He then picked up his cigarette and his eyes filled up with tears. He reached into his pocket and pulled out a wad of cash. He put the cash in my hand and told me to buy my Mom something nice. He said she really deserved it. I knew at that moment that he still had feelings for her. I waited to hear it. I wanted to hear him say he was sorry for what he had done, but it never came. Not that it would have changed anything.

He didn't owe me an apology he owed it to my Mom. He owed her much more than that. I looked at the money. It was probably a few hundred dollars. I stayed a while longer to hear the bar crowd give their political opinions of the days' news events and when Tom wasn't looking, I slipped the money back into his coat, all except my twenty. You can't buy forgiveness. That was the last I ever saw of Tom and it was as close as I would ever come to hearing him say he was sorry. After seeing him that way, the heaviness of hatred escaped my body. I could no longer hate him. Life had served him a fate far worse than anything I could deliver.

I was in my early years of the military when mom called to say that Tom had committed suicide. I knew it hit her hard even though their relationship had been tumultuous and had ended years before. I must admit that I have visited his grave tucked away in a little cemetery hidden under a group of pine trees. I apologized for hating him and gave him forgiveness. To see how he destroyed himself made me hurt inside. To see his name etched in stone made me remember the times when he was a good person. To see the letter his daughter had left by his stone brought out the tears. I wonder what ever happened to her.

CHAPTER 5

Big Mistake

I'm not even sure how to start this part of my story except to give you an understanding of what was going on in the world at the time that it happened. I've never made it public knowledge so I will say that this chapter is a confession; moreover, a skeleton that I feel needs to be let out.

In 1982, one of the most notable and unsolved crimes of our time happened. A paperboy named Johnny Gosch disappeared from his paper route while delivering papers one early morning in Des Moines. In 1984, another paperboy named Eugene Martin disappeared from his paper route as well, again in Des Moines. Also during this time, one of the most notorious criminals in our country was on a crime spree of monstrous proportions. His name was John Wayne Gacy. He was finally arrested for the murder of 33 boys, most of whom he buried under his house. What people don't know about Gacy is that his child molesting days began in Waterloo, Iowa in the 1970s.

About the time I had left Iowa for the start of my military service, a kid named Paul Bonnaci was telling his story. It's one of the most unbelievable stories I've ever heard; yet I believe every word. Paul told authorities that his sexual abuse started around the age of eight. He claims to have been abused by men in positions of high power. He talks of flying around the country to parties with high ranking politicians and the prominent circles of people that surround them. He tells of unspeakable acts between adults and kids and continues with tales of murder and rape, but the most shocking thing that Paul ever said was his confession that he was present when Johnny Gosch was kidnapped.

Another child to tell his story was a friend of Paul Bonacci. His name was Troy Bonner. He told horrific tales the same as Bonacci and implicated two prominent figures in his accusations. The first was Paul Baer who, at that time, was a well-known publisher. Troy told of many trips that he took with Baer. Places like Des Moines and numerous trips to Baer's residence in Council Bluffs, Iowa.

Several children came forward to complain about inappropriate behavior on the part of the second prominent figure implicated. His name was Lawrence E. King and he was the head of the Franklin Credit Union in Omaha, Nebraska. His political star was on the rise and he had solidified a place within the GOP. The children continued to talk. Bonacci told of trips he had taken with King to Sioux City, Iowa and to Chicago under the guise of political fund raising in the late 1980s. Lawrence King was high enough on the political totem pole to cover things up, but when the accusations against him continued to mount, the government stepped in. It was at this time that the Feds busted the doors down to the Franklin Credit Union under allegations of embezzlement on King's part. This is when the full scope of the child abuse came to light with the seizure of evidence from the credit union offices.

Even with all this making news, very little of it made the front headlines. Most of it disappeared from the public eye. The Discovery Channel made a documentary exposing what was known as the Franklin Cover Up. The film, titled *The Conspiracy Of Silence* exploited the scandal and all of the political figures involved, but when it was made public that the film was going to air, the government put the squeeze on the cable industry. If the film went public, the government was prepared to put severe restrictions on the industry, costing millions. The cable companies dropped the show and copies were to be destroyed. Again, it isn't hard to see the depth and scope of a child pornography ring tucked away in the heartland of America.

People do not understand how the world of child pornography works. We all think of child pornography as something on the internet, but in 1983, its roots sprouted from such places like Boys Town in Nebraska and the small towns of Iowa, Illinois, and Minnesota. So how did one go about buying the services of a child in 1983? At that time, all you needed was money and the desire. It wasn't hard to find someone who had those kinds of contacts. It was the same in the 1930's when prohibition was being enforced. People found the liquor. So if you wanted the services of a twelve year old boy with blonde hair and blue eyes, you just had to find one of those contacts. He would, in turn, contact what is known as a freelancer. The freelancer's job was to find prospective kids that fit that description and photograph them. The photos were compiled in catalogs and shown to the client for approval. The whole process was known as a "scavenger hunt." If the client decided that one of the children in the photos was what he was looking for, it was the freelancer's job to obtain the child as he saw fit. A kidnapping at an amusement park? A break-in and kidnapping at the child's house? Were Johnny Gosch and Eugene Martin previously sought out and photographed for a prospective client? Will we ever know?

So how do I come privy to such info? Well, even though I was aware of the disappearance of Johnny Gosch and the arrest of John Wayne Gacy, none of that crossed my mind when, at fifteen, I was asked to pose nude for a man and his camera. Most people would immediately say "No!" but my reaction was "you want me to do what?!" and he followed it up with, "I'll pay you one hundred dollars an hour to pose nude for me for pictures." One hundred dollars an hour wasn't chump change to a fifteen-year old kid in 1983 especially if you could make it in an hour.

I was approached at school one day by a guy in my grade. I'll call him Raymond. He asked me if I would be interested in making a lot of money. It was well-known that this kid was a juvenile delinquent. He quit school in the eighth grade. I never trusted him and never really liked him. The word "money" got my attention, however, and I listened to what he had to say. Raymond told me how he was making lots of money posing nude for a guy and his camera. Some guy who he called Paul. I agreed to meet this Paul guy. He was going to pick us up at Raymond's house.

Raymond seemed normal enough to me even though he had the worst reputation in town for boys his age. I would guess he was sixteen or seventeen. No one really knew because he had been held back in school a few times. We had a normal conversation as we sat on his weight bench in the basement of his house. At one point, his brother, who I also did not trust or like, came down and joined the conversation.

When Paul showed up, we climbed into his car. They struck up conversation like two good friends, but I have no idea how long they had known each other since he never talked about his relationship with Paul.

Paul's car was a compact four-door, like a Chevette or a Citation. He was cordial to me, but I could tell his mind was preoccupied. The drive was less than an hour. I have tried to remember the exact location where Paul took us and I have driven those roads hundreds of times trying to jar my memory, but I truly do not know. I remember the trailer where he had his photo studio. I remember it vividly. The outside was 1950's pastel green and white. It was a singlewide trailer. The photo studio was behind a partition. There was stuff everywhere except where the pictures were actually being taken. He used a sheet for a backdrop and he had lots of props to simulate bondage style photos. There were boxes and boxes of young boys' pictures. He was proud of those and even showed some of them to me. Though I never saw it, he told me that this was where he got the photos for his catalog.

That first time, Paul made few requests except that we undress and pose for pictures. He wasn't specific about any poses. He had us do some photos together, but again very non-specific. It lasted about an hour and then we were back in Paul's car headed for Camanche. I was carrying a fresh one hundred dollar bill. I had no reservations about the nude photos. They were only photos. Who cared? It was about the money. I guess that's the same attitude a prostitute has.

Paul was an unattractive, portly man, about five feet eight inches tall. He had balding gray-whitish hair that was always a bit disheveled and combed to the side. He always wore a windbreaker styled jacket and dress pants that ended above his belly-button. He still lived with his mom and on more than one occasion he met her halfway between his trailer and her house that sat just to the left and behind the trailer. She was always hollering for him and he would always go up to the house to satisfy her request. Paul was an unusually quiet character and a bit mild mannered, but he had an explosive side to him that I had the misfortune of being introduced to.

My second meeting with Paul was more of the same with the exception of the types of photos he took. He had us doing bondage style photos this time. Lots of ropes coupled with expressions of pain on our faces. He even entwined a broomstick under and over our arms. It was definitely weird, but again, I could care less. If this was the kind of photo he wanted, big deal, pay me! And pay me he did…another cool hundred in my pocket. When it came time to go home, Paul pulled me aside. He explained to me that he knew some people that were interested in meeting me. He said they liked muscular guys like me and said that one of them had commented about me. Obviously, Paul had been shopping my pictures around. He suggested that I meet him alone for a photo shoot stating that he would pay me one hundred and fifty dollars for the hour. He wanted me to go out into the woods and shoot outdoor photos. He continued saying that he wanted to use me in a porno film. He said he thought I was right for the part. I said I'd think about it.

Raymond never mentioned that Paul had approached him with anything like that before so it struck me as way out of the norm. I never told him what Paul said though. Before the third meeting with Paul, the two of us were sitting in the basement again just chewing the fat, when out of the blue

Raymond said in a rather hesitant arrangement of words, "I'm thinking that we should crack Paul upside his head and take his money." Now this was the kid I knew, this was what his reputation was built on. Bold, brazen criminal thinking and it's the exact reason why I didn't trust him. I wasn't sure what to say at this point. If I didn't go along with him, would he try to do the same to me? He had one of those mini baseball bats that you get at the minor league ball games. He was holding it in his right hand and smacking it in the center of his left. I could see Clinton Giants printed on the bat. I was out of my league now. There was something about the relationship between him and Paul that wasn't being made knowledgeable to me. Looking back now, I think Raymond was recruiting kids for Paul and Paul was promising things that he wasn't delivering on. I was sought out for a reason. Paul was looking for a muscular teen boy and Raymond delivered it. Maybe Paul wasn't paying extra for the head hunting services that he was providing. Who knows? Whatever it was, was enough to make him break out his souvenir bat in the hopes of taking a crack at Paul's noggin.

So what does a kid with little sense say to a kid with absolutely no sense in this situation? "How much money do you think he has?" I asked. When tasked with the responsibility of being a crisis manager, that's the best I could do. I can still hear myself saying it and watching the criminal's eyes light up with excitement at the thought of having an accomplice.

"He's got lots!" he exclaimed. Paul did have money. He kept it in rolls and when he peeled off our cash payment, I could see how thick that roll was. Looking back, I would venture to say he had at least a thousand dollars at any one time and he always kept it in his front pocket.

"What's he going to do to us?" Raymond asked. "He can't go to the police." He was right about that. Paul was very well aware of what could happen to him if we talked. Maybe that's why he kept so much money around. A good supply of hush money can soften a tough situation especially when you're dealing with two teenagers.

"I don't know, I don't want to go to jail," I answered.

"I'm not going to kill him," he fired back. "Just knock him out and take the money." About that time Paul came from around the corner. He pulled up to the curb and opened the passenger door from the inside. I climbed in back and lay down so that no one would recognize me. I didn't sit up until we were almost at Paul's trailer.

For lack of a solid plan or lack of courage, whatever the reason, the mini bat was left behind and the conversation was kept to a minimum while we rode to Paul's place. As the car came around the curve in the road, the trailer and the lot on which it sat came into view.

We climbed out of the car and Paul hurried us inside. He paid Raymond almost immediately and sent him back to the car. He then came over and asked if I had thought about making the movie. I said I didn't have a problem with it, but I wanted to see the girls that were going to be in it. He replied that he needed to see me perform while he took pictures. According to him, it was the first step to making an adult film. He wanted to be sure that I was right for the part. If everything went well, then he would let me pick the girls and we would do the film. All of fifteen and here was my shot at making the big screen. How cool was this? Being naïve should be a crime for everyone involved. I was the big perch and I took the bait. About halfway through my photo shoot

Paul attacked me. He threw himself on me and when I tried to fight him off, he became intensely angry!

"What do you think I'm paying you for?" he screamed. His faced changed into a deep red color. I was terrified. I couldn't get off the table that I was on. He had me pinned! Then suddenly, he eased up. He knew there would be consequences if he did something stupid. When he calmed down, he told me to get dressed. He reached into his pocket and gave me two hundred dollars and then motioned for me to go out to the car. I climbed in back wishing I had that mini bat. I think the other kid knew what had happened, maybe it had happened to him, but there wasn't a word spoken on the drive back to Camanche.

That was the last trip I made to Paul's place. He sought me out one day while he was driving around the school grounds. He made a quasi apology for what had happened and tried to convince me to go back to his trailer with him. I refused. I knew what he was capable of. Could I have been the next boy in Iowa to disappear? In my mind, it was not unlikely. I think once Paul had his assurance that I hadn't told and wouldn't tell anyone, he was able to leave without regret. He had committed a crime and for all I knew, he had committed it many times before and I'm sure many times after. I never saw Paul or Raymond again.

Years later, I was surfing the web to see whatever happened with the investigations of Johnny Gosch and Eugene Martin. It was then that I stumbled on to another missing person's case. A boy named Jacob Wetterling. He was abducted at gunpoint in 1989 in the town of St. Joseph, Minnesota. He was with his brother and another friend when it happened. The abductor held the kids and asked their ages. After their responses, he let two of them go and disappeared with Jacob. I could feel my deepest darkest secret opening the closet door. I continued to read and my heart beat faster.

Some of the people in Jacob's home town told investigators of a stranger that they had seen earlier in the day and they described him as 6ft tall, large build and receding white hair. They also had that particular man driving a small compact car. Sound familiar? My jaw fell open! That's how I would have described Paul. Was he capable of that? Absolutely. This was the first time that I had ever given thought to contacting the authorities in the hopes of bringing Paul to justice. That whole ordeal was mine to bear and I'm not sure what may have compelled me to make that decision. I had struggled with it for years, not so much because of what happened to me, but I felt that if I had said something then, maybe other kids wouldn't have suffered because of him. Paul would never stop. He was harboring a demon inside and it had to be fed. Guys like Paul don't have the ability to control such a thing. John Wayne Gacy didn't have the ability. It's a compulsion that they can't control.

The following morning I called the FBI in the state of Iowa. I have no idea why I picked them and as with many governmental agencies, I received absolutely no help and no guidance. The guy on the phone basically blew me off, telling me that "it had happened twenty years ago and the guy was probably dead now anyway." I realized then what I was up against and knew that I wasn't going to get much help in the matter.

I called Jacob's father Jerry and talked to him on the phone. I told him my story and he put me in touch with the detective who was heading up the investigation. As expected, I got the same response as I did from the FBI.

"Your guy isn't the guy were looking for," she said. "The picture you saw was an artist's sketch." I never saw a sketch; I was going by the description that I had read.

My next course of action was to contact the Department of Public Safety in Des Moines, Iowa. It took over a year to have an investigator email and tell me to file a formal complaint with the local law enforcement in my hometown. That's laughable, but it's my only recourse at this time and it's probably the only chance I have of ever locating the other kid involved. He may hold more pieces to the puzzle. He would certainly remember the location of the trailer, which would lead authorities to a positive identification of Paul and his whereabouts, if in fact he's still living.

I want to bring Paul to justice for the simple reason that I have to live with the fact that I didn't say anything and because of my actions other kids surely suffered. I can only hope that they didn't endure a worse fate than what I did. There isn't a day that goes by that I don't see a young child and think to myself how easy it would be for someone to make them disappear forever. Truth be known, it was a big reason for me not to have children. I wouldn't be able to withstand the mental anguish of that very thought. I lay awake at night thinking that I should have told someone and I beat myself up over the whole thing. I don't blame anyone except myself. I'm simply seeking closure.

CHAPTER 6

High School

As I put the Paul episode deep into the closet, I moved on into high school. Gone were the days of the neighborhood baseball and football games. Most of the kids were preparing themselves for college. I never really considered college. High School was a chore for me and I couldn't see spending another four years of my life for a piece of paper. Jeff was still the king of truancy and deep down I secretly wished I could've been there with him, but it wasn't meant to be for me. It wasn't that I enjoyed high school. Every kid has his reasons for not liking it and my reason was simple. I felt more and more isolated as I progressed towards graduation. Jeff and I didn't see each other during the school hours. I enrolled in what was known as Multi-Occupational Curriculum. I worked half the day and went to school during the other half. It was the only way I was going to be able to continue to pay for my gym membership and afford my own car. It also lessened the time spent inside those school walls and still enabled me to accumulate credits.

Along with the feeling of isolation, high school also delivered the daunting task of living in my brother's shadow. He was the quintessential perfect student. He carried straight 'A's and played every sport. He was state champion in tennis and was beloved by the faculty. I was just the opposite. More than once I endured the you-should-be-more-like-your-brother speech from them. I did keep good grades though, as that was one of Mom's requests.

I could have done well in scholastic sports, but I was deep into bodybuilding by this time. The coaches, who were both P.E. teachers, greatly resented me for not participating. I endured verbal abuse from both of them regularly most of it stemming from my desire to become a bodybuilder. They also resented the fact that my parties were instrumental reasons for the class jocks breaking the rules when it came to drinking. I endured what they dished out knowing that it wouldn't last forever.

Jeff and I began experimenting with drugs and alcohol during our freshmen year. We became famous for our abilities to find or create a party. The greatest party we ever threw happened when my mom decided to go to Chicago for the weekend. Jeff and I drove into Clinton to buy beer. We went to our usual place, which was a rundown corner store on the North end of town. The store itself probably should have been condemned, but teenaged drunkenness wasn't about to be deterred by some health or building code violation. The legal drinking age then was eighteen and Jeff definitely looked it. He never got carded.

"Do you think two kegs will do?" he asked.

"Yeah I think so," I replied. "I'm guessing maybe thirty people."

We dropped the deposit on the counter and loaded the kegs into the car. I was confident that we were going to have a nice Friday night get together with some of our closest friends. I couldn't have been further from the truth.

The sun hadn't been down for more than fifteen minutes when cars started filling up the parking lot in the park behind my house. I peeked out to see the kids coming from every direction. The house filled quickly, but the kids kept coming.

The beer ran out within the first hour and panic surged through the crazed teen crowd. Jeff ran out to the gas station where one of our friends worked and bought all the beer he could carry. It didn't take long before it was time for another run. This time I jumped in my car and set out on the errand. I had to stop by a girl's house in Clinton anyway as she needed a ride to the party. Her mom was implementing a curfew that night and she had to shimmy down the drainpipe from the second story to sneak out. She climbed in the car dressed to kill in designer jeans and a hairstyle that had her hair poofed out and loaded with hairspray. She could have been in a Whitesnake video. I was smiling from ear to ear.

We drove back to Camanche with a car full of beer. As we turned the corner onto my street, I saw four police cars parked in front of my house!

"Isn't that your house?" she asked.

"That was my house," I replied.

"Aren't you going to stop?" she questioned.

"Are you out of your mind? We've got enough beer in this car to get the whole town drunk and I'm not eighteen!" I answered. We continued to drive around Camanche until I was sure that the police had moved on.

By the time we got back to the party, most of the kids had left at the request of law enforcement. Now before I left, I gave Jeff the dubious task of making sure the house wasn't destroyed. He failed miserably.

The house smelled like pot and the basement carpet was soaked with beer. There was a six inch hole in the bathroom wall and someone vomited on the floor. I didn't find that till the aroma drifted into the hallway. The culprit was kind enough to cover it up with the bath rug. My date looked at me.

"You're in big trouble," she said

"Where is Jeff?" I hollered.

"He's in the bedroom."

I tracked him down and found him passed out on my mom's bed.

I began cleaning up one room at a time and finally started kicking people out. As I made my way to the basement it dawned on me that these jackals had probably drank every ounce of liquor stored in Mom's bar. Her stash was small and all the bottles were covered with dust. Mom wasn't a drinker, but if she saw empty bottles, I would get the blame, so I filled them back up with water and food dye.

I did manage to clean the house and repair the bathroom wall. Mom would have never found out had it not been for an ex-girlfriend who ratted me out with a letter. All said and done, I spent a very long time being grounded.

Around this time, Mom started dating Marc. I liked him because he wasn't a father figure by any means. He was just one of the guys. As much as that was ok with me, it didn't settle well with mom. Marc was a big kid. He was laid off from Caterpillar and from what I could see; he had no intention of finding another job. He loved hunting and trapping and more importantly to him, he loved the bar life. League pool and beer, and not to be diminished by any of this, was his love for drag racing. He had been very successful in the racing arena at one time, but racing needs one thing, one constant thing to make it successful and that's a steady flow of cash. You don't get that being a member of the unemployment line. I know mom had financially supported his hobby for some time and I'm sure that caused a great deal of strain in their relationship. At any rate, Marc and I got along very well. We shot pool at the local bar and he took me hunting and trapping whenever I wanted to go. Like I said, he was just one of the guys. So what was the defining moment of life with Marc? Oddly enough, it was his near exit.

I had come home for lunch from school. I only had a half hour to eat and get to work at the factory. Mom, if she was home, usually made me something or packed me a sandwich, but not today. She was busy throwing Marc's belongings out into the front lawn.

All his guns and racing trophies laid strewn about in the yard. As I approached the house, I could see that she had filled the garage as well. Oh man, where was Jerry Springer? The white trash flag was flying high in the neighborhood! The reason? Another case of infidelity. I just hung my head. How much more must my mom endure? I wanted to just wrap my arms around her and give her a big hug, but she was on a tirade. She had already been to hell and back and from what I was witnessing, she had just purchased a return ticket. It was like we were being punished when it came to a stable home life. Marc certainly didn't give us stability, but I got the impression that if he had had a steady job, things between mom and him would have been better.

Deep down it hurt to see Mom back in this same old situation. She didn't deserve this. She was out breaking her back to see that we had everything we needed. She was certainly entitled to some sort of stability in her relationship. Maybe she had a certain amount of gullibility in her that guys picked up on. I never saw her as such. She was always so strong in my eyes until the day she nearly booted Marc out. That's the first time I saw her vulnerability peek through. She was so very strong. She worked in the factory in a man's world and I know the guys there didn't treat her right, but she never let it show. She never brought it home with her. For all the good that she did for us, her reward was guys like Marc. It was so unfair. I think she was clinging onto the hope that Marc would eventually get a job and things would change, but it was just hope floating in the wind.

High school was becoming a downer. I knew life was closing in. Jeff had gone to boot camp the summer of our junior year. He had joined the Army, and once he finished his senior year, he would be leaving. I envied that move. It was both bold and brilliant.

My senior year was even worse than my junior year. My brother had gone to college. We weren't close, a fact I attribute to our being so totally different. All that aside, he was still my brother and when he was home, the puzzle was complete. After he left for college, the house became hollow. Bodybuilding isolated me even more, both at school and at home. Even at that age, pumping iron was an addiction. I was always working out so by the time I came home, dinner was sitting on the stove waiting for me to reheat it. I ate alone on many occasions and secretly wished someone, anyone, would pull up a chair. My sister and I were four years apart. It might as well have been forty when you're a teenager. You can't drag your little sister to a beer bash. Everyone in the neighborhood was preparing for life after high school.

I knew my future was not going to be Camanche, Iowa. The prospect of working my life away in a factory for the next forty years just wasn't something I intended to do. My only option was the military and I soon found myself standing in the doorway of the United States Army Recruiter.

"Come on in," he bellowed. His uniform crackling with every step as the starch gave way at the creases. His chest was loaded down with the weight of badges and ribbons and tassels. This guy's uniform was immaculate.

"What can I do for you?" he continued.

"I want to join the Army."

"Have a seat," he commanded as he grabbed his pen and paper.

"So, what do you want to do?" he asked.

I had no clue. I had visions of jumping out of airplanes and swimming in swamp water with a knife clenched between my teeth, my face painted with camouflage.

"I need helicopter mechanics," he stated half twisted into a question as if to steer my mind in a purposeful direction. I couldn't even find the oil dipstick on my car and admittedly ran the transmission out of fluid because I didn't know you had to check it. Now this guy wanted me to become a mechanic on a helicopter? All my visions turned from jumping out of an airplane to a helicopter crashing in the jungle because I forgot to check the oil. This guy was a gambler and he was risking a lot if he was going to put me in that job. He spruced up the deal by telling me that I could go overseas and I could get guaranteed promotions and I would only have to join for two years. Oh it was sounding good for sure!

"Listen, you think about it, I'm going out to grab a bite to eat, when I get back, if you're still interested, we'll draw up the paperwork." He swaggered out the door leaving me with a feeling of awe.

As I sat there considering my options, a Marine Corps recruiter who had overheard my interest poked his head in the door. He was big and bold and his uniform was far and away more gorgeous than the Army officer who had just left. He walked to the doorway of his office; looked left, and then right and when he figured that the coast was clear, he put his best sales pitch to work on me.

"Son, are you thinking about joining the military?" he asked. He didn't even wait for an answer. "Step in here and let me show you what the United States Marine Corps is all about and what we can do for you," he finished. I gravitated toward his office. Boy, did I want to be in that uniform!

I was knowledgeable now. The Army had told me what I wanted to do in life so when the man in blue asked, I was ready. I was talking the talk and walking the walk. "I want to be a helicopter mechanic," I spouted.

"No kidding!" he exclaimed. "I need mechanics bad."

"I want to see the world," I continued.

"How about Japan?" he countered. He was a salesman and he had an answer for everything. He knew how to play the game. Rook to your bishop. He let me believe that I was running the negotiation; helicopters and Japan and guaranteed rank. It was going to have to be a six-year hitch if I wanted all that. Six years traveling the world, or the next forty in the factory. Alex, I'll take 'What is a no-brainer' for a thousand.

When the Army recruiter returned, it was too late. I had been brainwashed by the man in that unbelievable uniform. The paperwork was drawn up.

"So did you think about our deal?" he asked.

"Sorry, I'm going to be a Marine!" I replied and I strolled out of there dreaming of the day when that uniform would drape over me. Checkmate.

The recruiter met me at my house a few days later since I wasn't old enough to sign the contract on my own. It would need Mom's blessing to become more than ink on paper. She had her reservations, but in the end she signed it.

I had joined in the delayed entry program, which meant that I had up to a year to report for duty and I would meet with my recruiter one weekend a month in preparation for boot camp.

The weekends with the recruiter were boys being boys weekends. Drinking beer, shooting pool, and talking about what was going to happen to us at boot camp. School was flying by so fast that when the month of May rolled around, I was asking, "What just happened here?" My date for boot camp was two weeks before my actual high school graduation so I found myself in the principal's office asking if I could get my diploma early. He reached into his desk drawer, thumbed through a stack of diplomas, removed mine from the masses and signed it right there. No congratulations, no best of luck; nothing. I would have settled for a "Now get out of my office," but it wasn't to be. I walked out of the high school alone leaving a handful of close friends and an empty locker.

CHAPTER 7

Boot Camp

The United States Marine Corps; Uncle Sam's Misguided Children. Or better put, Boy Scouts without Adult Supervision. The first step other than signing my life away was a weekend at MEPS. Military Entrance Processing Station…aka, The Hall of Lies. They lie to you about how life in the Marine Corps will be and you lie to them about what a model citizen you are. It's a classic tit for tat chess game. It's also an all day physical followed by more paperwork and an oath.

At one point during the arduous process of filling out papers, this viciously mean gunnery sergeant leaned over his desk and stared me right in the eyes and asked, "Have you ever smoked dope?"

"No, Sir!" I replied.

He repeated the question again and followed it with "maybe you didn't hear me."

Again I replied, "No, Sir!" I wasn't going to buckle.

He glared at me. He knew I was lying, but his tactics weren't going to get me to admit to it. He read me the riot act along with the penalties if he later found out that I was lying to him. I paid him no mind.

The other guys that made those weekend get-togethers with the recruiter were all on the same plane as me. It was a comfortable feeling to say the least. We were all from small towns in Iowa and that alone fortified our bond. Deep down we knew we would have to stick together to get through boot camp. The plane ride to San Diego was a solemn one and I didn't feel the sting of reality until we deplaned and met the Marine Liaison in the airport. The recruiter in Iowa elected one out of the fifteen or so recruits to carry all the paperwork. When we were standing in front of the Liaison, the recruit plopped the paperwork down on the podium.

"You have three seconds to pick up that paperwork or I'll split your gourd wide open!" he barked. The words danced in my head. It was a death threat spewed out in a hushed tone so that only we could hear it. Fear overcame every one of us in an instant.

"Get on that bus outside! If I hear one word out of any of you, I'm going to come out there and smash your heads! Now move!" he hollered.

I don't know how many people I trampled to get on that bus, but I wasn't about to be the last one on board. We sat on the bus for thirty minutes waiting for more recruits. When the Liaison was sure that we had everyone, the doors closed and we rumbled out onto the interstate outside San Diego's Lindberg Airport. We must have driven well over an hour, which didn't make sense, as the Marine Corps Recruit Depot is right next to the airport. Later, I found out that they do that in case anyone has second thoughts and tries to make a break for it, they'll think the airport is too far away.

The bus arrived at the depot and the longest night of my life began. "Get off this bus you maggots and get on those yellow footprints! Last one out is mine! Now move!" he cried out with spit flying in all directions. I jumped on the first set of yellow footprints that I could find and snapped to attention.

They filed us into building after building. First stop was the barber shop, then the clothing issue, then toiletries and bed linens and finally a big bag to put it all in. We looked like a bunch of misfits with our bald heads, baggy clothes and untied shoelaces. It was 2:00 a.m. before we actually put our heads down on a pillow. I remember lying there, rubbing my head, giggling with the guy above me wondering what I had just gotten myself into. The guy above me was Armstrong. He was from Iowa as well and he didn't seem to be taking this as serious as the rest of us. His laissez-faire attitude put me at ease and we became good friends.

The sleep was short. We managed all of two hours before it came to a screeching halt with a drill instructor clanging a garbage can at 4:00 a.m. Armstrong almost fell off the top bunk; his eyes weren't even open. Guys were digging in their sea bags to find things that they had bundled up and stuffed inside just hours before.

"You got three minutes to get outside and get ready for chow!" said a voice from the front of the squad bay.

We were a humble bunch at best. Each of us carried a flashlight in our hand as it was pitch black and we mobbed ourselves into some sort of formation in front of the barracks. The drill instructor blatantly showed his disgust as he greeted us.

"You guys are the worst bunch of scum bags I've seen yet! You four right there, yeah you, you don't look as dumb as the rest, get up front!" he hollered selecting the ones who would lead us. I wasn't one of the four.

The first week of boot camp was more paperwork, physicals, shots, glasses and testing; hours and hours of testing. It was like the Iowa Basic Scholastic Tests all over again! Surprisingly, the drill instructor called it right when he said we were a bunch of dummies. I made the top twenty-five in the testing arena, which was a sure sign that the others weren't very smart. I was given a chance to go to Annapolis. That's right; they offered me, the kid who pulled a "D" in geometry, the Naval Academy. The catch? Two years of Naval Academy prep school followed by four years at the academy and then a six-year hitch. The reason I was here in the first place was because I didn't want to go to school so why would I consider another six years of it? Hindsight is 20/20. I've never been one to look back at missed opportunities and it's a good thing given how many of them I've had. Life doesn't move in reverse. You make a decision and follow it through and that's what I did. I flat out told them, "No thanks."

I moved on into boot camp like a man on a mission. I was in great shape and I handled everything they threw at me, but that doesn't mean I liked it. I would be hard pressed to find anything about boot camp that was completely enjoyable, but there were a few things that I didn't mind. One thing I didn't mind was marching. The songs, the rhythm, the cadence; to me it was soothing, but like anything, too much of a good thing was just that; too much. We marched relentlessly! We marched to class, to the chow hall, to the barracks; it never ceased. I lived for Sundays and that precious hour before bedtime. That was when we had time to talk amongst ourselves and write letters home and wash off the stench that had infested our bodies from a long day in the sun. On Sundays, we had two choices, go to church or stay in the barracks and do your laundry. I'm not a religious guy and I wasn't about to go without clean clothes.

The Marine Corps' strategy worked on most of the guys in our platoon. It was simple. Break them down, and then build them up. They successfully turned us into trained and disciplined killers. I had absolutely no fear whatsoever when I graduated. That's what they instilled within us, complete and total invincibility.

Drill instructors have uncanny ways to make you fear them. It's a necessary process of the training. Fear commands respect. We fell for it for the first few weeks, but once we had them figured out, we realized that all we had to do was go through the motions and we would make it to the end. You had to be mentally and physically strong of course, or you'd never make it. They would weed you out.

The first month was by far the worst. We were being taught the life of a Marine. Make your bunk, fold your socks, yes sir, no sir and we were learning how to drill. We were absolutely horrible at drill! Every platoon is during their first month. We drilled every day rain or shine. If it rained, we just pushed the bunks to one side of the squad bay and drilled indoors. "Present, Arms! Right shoulder, Arms!" I can still hear it. I hated that rifle. That thing weighed 7.6 pounds, but by the end of the day, it might as well have been seventy six pounds.

By the second month we were becoming a well-oiled unit. It was combat training time. We left the confines of the recruit-training depot and moved to Camp Pendleton. This is where the drill instructors showed their bad side. Some were prone to drink when the sun went down and upon their return to the barracks, many recruits suffered physical abuse as a result. I witnessed a recruit taking a shot to the stomach from a DI who wasn't even part of our platoon. We were far and away from the spit shine of MCRD. There was no supervision over the drill instructors here and they exploited that fact at every turn.

Camp Pendleton was where we learned to shoot our rifles with deadly accuracy. The rifle range was another part of the Marine Corps that I didn't care for. Two full weeks of rifle training with the first week doing nothing, but sitting in different positions with an empty rifle. The rifle was and is the essence of being a Marine. We were killers. We were being trained with American tax dollars to protect the freedoms that had been given to us by those who had fought and served before us. The rifle is the key to protecting freedom. If you couldn't march, they found other things for you to do. If you couldn't run, they found other things for you to do, but if you couldn't kill another human being from eight hundred yards away, you would be going home. You were not worthy of the title "Marine," plain and simple.

We returned to MCRD only to suffer the dreaded mess hall duty. It was only one week long, but considered to be the worst week in boot camp. I averaged, at best, five hours of sleep a day during that week. There were no letters home, no mail calls, and more than once I skipped showering. They were pushing me to my physical limits. Up at 3:00 a.m. and back to the barracks at 9:00 p.m. It was grueling to say the least. The only time I sat down was when it was time to eat. By the time mess duty ended, I was counting the days till graduation.

When the third and final month of training came around, we were starting to feel like full-fledged Marines. We marched like pros and our rifle drill was clean and crisp. By now we had our drill instructors figured out. We had a total of four, and out of the four, there were only two worth mentioning and both of them were buffoons. Neither had rhythm when they called our marching cadence, which made it difficult to stay in step and painful to the ear. They had one thing in common though and that was the ability to provide us with non-stop comedy. Of course, none of it was intentional, but I guess humor, much like beauty, is in the eye of the beholder.

The junior of the two was named Pendelton. He was a real life Barney Fife. He looked and acted just like him! We all knew it was his first platoon as a drill instructor. It showed like Rudolph's red nose.

As a recruit, the one thing we never had enough of was food and many of us resorted to stuffing our pockets with crackers and snacks from the chow hall. Of course, this was against the rules so we had to eat our treasured morsels under the cover of darkness. Barney Fife would tiptoe between the bunks to see if he could catch someone eating and when he thought he had his victim, the speech, which was whispered, went like this, "I know you're eating, I can hear you unwrapping something. Let me catch you, I'll make you run an extra five miles. I smell something over here. Don't act like you can't hear me!" When he said it to me, I would feign asleep and even throw in a fake snore. "I'm not fooled!" he would say between clenched teeth. Then, at the sound of more unwrapping from across the squad bay, he would turn and run to the other side in the hopes of catching someone else. I could feel the bunk shaking from Armstrong's laughter.

The other guy was Skipp. He was carrying way too much stress and was in dire need of a vacation. He looked like a constipated Opie Taylor. His eyes were fixed in a permanent squint, which only accentuated his ghostly white face and freckles. Skipp never failed to provide us with great comedy.

The last ten minutes before bed were spent standing in front of our bunks waiting for the DI to perform his nightly hygiene inspections. On this particular night, we were also tasked with the dubious duty of washing our M-16 rifle slings. Our final rifle inspection was the following day. Not to be outdone in order of importance, we were also required to show that we could tie our dress uniform ties during this evening's inspection. We were a week away from graduation and we were getting cocky.

There was a guy in the platoon named Orsini. He was a little on the chubby side and kind of looked like Tony Danza. He was always making us laugh and he knew how to get the best of Skipp. While Skipp was making his rounds, Orsini tied his rifle sling into a perfect double Windsor necktie knot and hung it around his neck. He looked so proud standing there in his boxer shorts. It was all I could do not to laugh when the inevitable happened.

"You think you're so funny huh, Orsini?!" he screamed in his face. "Just get on the floor and start the push-ups," he barked.

Orsini fell to the floor with a smirk on his face and began the push-ups. Skipp finished his inspections and returned to the exhausted Orsini. He reached down and picked him up by the sling that was still around his neck and then, he looped it over Orsini's bunk. Poor Orsini was short, much shorter than the top bunk and he was now standing on his tiptoes gasping for air. His face was turning blue! Skipp started in with the razzing.

"You're a funny guy, Orsini. Who thinks Orsini's funny? Raise your hand," he hollered across the squad bay still forcing Orsini up on his toes.

We could hear him choking as he struggled to get loose while Skipp continued screaming in his face. Finally, Skipp had his fill and released the sling. Orsini fell to his knees. After the lights went out, I could hear Orsini giggling.

That same Orsini on the one and only day we had on-base liberty, sought out Skipp somewhere near the base theaters. Skipp was sitting at an umbrella table having a much-needed break drinking a soda when Orsini strolled over to him.

"Drill Instructor Sergeant Skipp, when this private graduates, he's going to buy you a beer, Sir," he announced.

Skipp looked up squinting into the sun and like every threat to emerge from a DI's mouth, he said in a hushed tone. "Orsini you're not going to graduate because I'm going to kill you first and if I fail to kill you, you better hope that I don't ever see you again because it will be my mission to hunt you down. Do you understand me, Orsini?"

"Sir, yes, sir!" he bellowed out grinning from ear to ear.

"Now get away from me before I lose all control!"

When the big day finally arrived, we were running around like girls at a slumber party. The excitement was unbearable. We had survived everything they threw at us. We were top dogs at MCRD on that day. It was our day to shine. The DI gave the command to fall out into formation. He looked at all of us and told us that we were about to hold the coveted title that we had all fought so hard to possess. We then started the march to the parade grounds. Our feet pounded the deck in unison, we hummed the musical cadence that the DI used to drive our feet, but above all of the din, was the pounding of our hearts. This was what is was all about.

We hit the parade deck in stride with all the other platoons that were graduating and we fell into our respective places facing the grandstand. I searched the faces for my mom and my sister, but the faces blended together like a Leroy Neiman painting. The speech being given by the commanding officer was nothing but noise, drowned out by the roar of a passing jet.

I continued to search the faces and I was still coming up empty. The DI turned to face us and barked his last command.

"Platoon dismissed!"

I did an abrupt about face and looked around at the guys that I would have given my life for. Marines were scattering in all directions. Orsini was looking for the elusive Skipp. I was looking for Armstrong. Where had he gone? In the mêlée, he had broken away from the masses and was getting into a cab.

"Armstrong!" I hollered.

He stopped and turned. "I have to go man, my flights leaving," he said.

My eyes watered up and my insides felt like I had just lost a best friend. The Marine Corps was cruel like that, always forcing people out of your life right when the friendship began to take hold.

"Yeah I know, man. Hey we had fun right? Maybe I'll catch up to you in Iowa someday," I rambled on.

"Take care," he said and the cab door closed.

Armstrong was in the reserves, which meant he was actually going home before he went off to school. This was just a part time gig for him, but for me, it was all I had. He was the one guy I had actually bonded with in boot camp and it ended like that. I never saw him again. I called him months later, but it was like two guys who didn't have anything to say to one another. I realized then that it was just a boot camp bond.

As I watched his cab drive off, I turned to see who else I could shake hands with. From the grand stand, I saw her approach. It was my mom. I gave her the biggest hug of my life. I hoped I had made her proud. If she only knew what I had gone through to get to that point. I looked at my sister and smiled. "Let's get out of here," I said with a grin.

CHAPTER 8

Marine Corps

Life after boot camp meant more schooling. I was going to be a helicopter mechanic no matter what. If I didn't pass the schools, I'd end up back at Camp Pendleton only this time as a ground-pounding "grunt." A term we used to describe that guy on the front line carrying that detested rifle. I did not endure the physical anguish of boot camp to have that happen to me. I never joined the Corps with the intent on staying until I retired. I enlisted for the sole purpose of obtaining a skill that would help me further down the road.

My first stop after San Diego was the Naval Air Station in Millington, Tennessee. Checking in was the classic Marine Corps "'Sorry, we are completely unorganized. Your school doesn't start for another two weeks.'" I spent those next two weeks cleaning the barracks, polishing floors and washing linens. I was roomed up with two other guys, both of whom were already in class.

This was the Marine Corps' equivalent of college and we acted accordingly. We played pranks on all the new guys by telling them we still had morning hygiene inspections that commenced at 5:00 a.m. and sure enough, at the stroke of five, they would be standing in the hallway in their boxers waiting for someone to come and inspect their freshly shaved faces. We'd follow that one up with "and don't forget the 6:00 a.m. formation march to the chow hall." When six rolled around, we'd rush to the window to see who fell for it and sure enough there would be at least five guys standing in front of the barracks in a make shift formation.

Tennessee is where I started working out again. They had a decent gym and I managed to get time to train. I also took up horseback riding, but both past times took a back seat to the actual purpose for me being there, and that was helicopter school.

I thought the schools were going to be intense and I was prepared to dig my heels in, but it never got to the point where I couldn't handle it. I applied myself, graduated top of my class, and was meritoriously promoted to the next rank. By now, I was pretty sure that I could handle this thing called helicopter maintenance, but it was the other stuff about the Marine Corps that was getting under my skin. The recruiter never said anything about weekly cleanings and room inspections and guard duty. What was this all about? His words were, "after boot camp, it's just like a job." I wasn't finding it to be exactly that.

Millington came and went and I soon found myself based at the Naval Air Station in Pensacola, Florida. I was here to attend Naval Air Crew Survival Training. This school alone was worth the eight years of service I gave this country. It was all about physical fitness and learning how to survive in the event that you found yourself behind enemy lines. There was no homework and no studying. All you had to do was show up and make an effort.

I had four roommates, some of whom I knew in Tennessee. After our school day was over, it was nothing but drinking and partying. We hung out at the club on the base that was located next to ours. That's where all the females were and consequently, that's where we always found trouble.

I'll admit I was never able to hold my liquor and I never knew when to slow down. When Friday night rolled around, we headed for the club. I hadn't been there for more than an hour before I was completely toasted. I tried everything in my bag of tricks to persuade a cute Navy girl to leave the club with me. She agreed, but during our exit at closing time, I lost her in the crowd. I stumbled my way over to the closest barracks building and walked in the front door. It just so happened to be the female barracks. This was definitely off limits to the guys. The female on guard duty told me to leave immediately. I wanted to, but I just didn't have the ability. I stumbled down the hallway.

It didn't take long for the sound of police sirens to get my attention. I scurried out the fire exit and ran for dear life! I dodged and weaved my way into the woods finally hiding in a bush. When the smoke had cleared and I was sure they were gone, I ventured out exiting the forest on the opposite side. I crossed a parking lot and came upon another set of barracks. I figured I would go in and have someone call me a cab. As I walked, the girl that I was supposed to have left the club with showed up. She invited me over to her room for the night.

When morning arrived, I rolled over and looked at the clock. It was 9:00 a.m. I jumped out of bed and into a cab. School started at seven. I arrived and was directed straight to the First Sergeant's office. He threatened me with the loss of my guaranteed contract and a promising career at Camp Pendleton making love to a rifle day in and day out. That was the last time I tipped the bottle while in the Corps.

After Pensacola, I landed in New River, North Carolina. Again, the Marine Corps was completely unprepared for my arrival. The advanced Helicopter Maintenance Course wasn't due to start for at least a month. In the interim, I became a member of the Squadron HMM-365. HMM stands for Helicopter Maintenance Medium; medium refers to the size of the helicopter. This was supposed to constitute a portion of my on-the-job training. It didn't live up to my expectations.

The guys there treated me like the new guy I was, many times going out of their way to exploit the fact that I didn't know anything about helicopters. I routinely got stuck with barracks duty and ended up shining floors all night. The Sergeant Major was a short guy who made a cigar part of his uniform. He didn't like me at all. He even denied my Christmas leave stating that since I didn't have any kids, I should let the guys who did, spend it with their families. I went over his head and got my request approved. By now I had realized that I had made a big mistake enlisting in the Marine Corps.

The guys in my class were great. The instructors even came out and partied with us on occasion. The class itself was like any Marine Corps School. It was set up for dummies and again I graduated with honors and another meritorious promotion. More importantly, it signified the end of my schooling. I was asked if I would consider staying with HMM-365 as they were short on personnel. I smiled and politely said, "No thanks," since my next stop was Japan.

When I set foot on the island of Okinawa, Japan, the Corps again failed to live up to its promises. American tax dollars had just trained me to be a helicopter mechanic, but now, the Master Sergeant in charge of things was telling me that I was going to be working in a warehouse.

Working that job did have its advantages. One of them being weekends off. The job was unbelievably boring. It was technically classified as IMRL, which stands for Individual Materials Readiness List. In short, it was a warehouse that housed goods that were being stored for the sole purpose of being shipped out to various units in the event of war. We kept things like maintenance test equipment and special tools. It was as exciting as watching paint dry. I was a babysitter of inanimate objects. IMRL at that time wasn't even an actual job listing on the Marine Corps' list of jobs.

There were five of us assigned to the warehouse and between the five of us, no one had a clue how to maintain inventory of the equipment. We were a three ring circus. We couldn't keep track of equipment that never left our possession!

The Corps assigned two guys to the warehouse in the hopes of getting a grip on an operation that, on paper, looked simple. The new HMFIC was Master Sergeant Cromwell. (HMFIC is a long acronym for man in charge). He was definitely the man for the job. He had a plan and he successfully executed it immediately.

The other guy that came in with the change of command was Gunnery Sergeant Lewis. He was a drinker and he loved to chase women. We spent days on the beach looking at girls and talking about retiring in the Philippines. Though rank dictated that he was my boss, he was also a close friend.

The warehouse job, for all of its negatives, allowed me to settle into a nine-to-five schedule, which let me concentrate on bodybuilding. Okinawa had a very nice fitness facility and I fell into a regular training routine.

My obsession with bodybuilding started in the third grade when I saw "Superstar" Billy Graham's picture on a muscle magazine. Throughout high school I competed in bodybuilding competitions that culminated with the Mr. Teen Iowa. My childhood dream was to make the pros. When I graduated from boot camp, I weighed one hundred and sixty pounds dripping wet. By the close of my short stint at New River, I was one hundred and eighty five pounds and dabbling with anabolic steroids. In 1985 it was legal and I was ordering steroids out of a catalog.

The island paradise of Okinawa was the home to many of the weightlifters on the Marine Corps' power lifting team. These guys were monstrous! I had never trained in a gym with guys that looked like this. It furthered my desire to get big.

After my first use of steroids in New River, the seed had been planted, but Okinawa posed a problem for me. I couldn't get the drugs through customs so I was going to have to find a connection on the island. I wasn't too concerned when I saw the size of the guys in the gym. Finding steroids is like anything else. If you're a smoker, you'll find cigarettes, if you're a drinker, you'll find alcohol and so it was that I found performance enhancing drugs in Okinawa.

The gym on Camp Butler was where the big boys trained and I made it my home. I had never seen a man bench-press six hundred pounds or squat one thousand pounds before, but I witnessed it all right there.

It took me a few months to find a source for the "juice," but it did happen courtesy of a Navy doctor and another guy who was weeks away from being discharged. This guy was married to a girl who was also in the service. He said he was going back to California to finish his out-processing with the military, but that he would be returning and staying until his wife was also discharged. He told me that he would bring back more drugs than I could imagine. He was true to his word.

People were starting to take notice that I was growing out of proportion. I had to apply for a medical waiver for the weight that I now was. The Marine Corps instilled a policy that stated one's height must be proportionate to their weight. At five foot six and two hundred and fifteen pounds, I did not fit that mold, but because my body fat percentage was low, the rule was waived. I was given a waiver that said I was allowed to weigh between two hundred and ten and two hundred and twenty pounds. If I got any heavier than that, I would have to go back to medical. It also gave me the privilege of not having to upkeep my uniform sizes. Most of the guys on the power lifting team only had two uniforms that fit in addition to their camouflaged ones.

What you should understand is that, while the Marine Corps publicly denounced the use of anabolic steroids, they didn't really care. There was no policy in place that dealt with steroid abuse. They didn't have the finances or the means to test for it. They also weren't going to take the chance of losing the inter-service power lifting meets to the Air Force or the Army. The Marine Corps liked guys like me to look the way we did. It fit the reputation and persona of being a Marine and they weren't about to change that.

When my tour was coming to a close, Gunny Lewis convinced me to stay on the island and finish out my time with the Corps right there in Paradise. It sounded like a good idea. He called the headquarters in Washington D.C. to find out where my next duty station was, in the hopes of having it changed. I could hear the voice on the other end of the phone, but I couldn't make out the words. Gunny wasn't saying anything. Then he looked at me and said, "Uh oh." He put the phone back up to his mouth. "He can't refuse those can he?" he asked. "Well, thanks anyway," he replied and hung up. He looked at me and shook his head.

"Well?" I asked.

"You're going to Quantico, Virginia. What did you do? Score high on some tests or something?" he asked.

"As a matter of fact, I did," I replied.

"You're supposed to flunk those things dummy!" he hollered. "I can't do anything for you. It'll take an act of Congress to get you out of those." He paused. "Quantico isn't the end of the world; just yours!" he laughed. I dropped my head.

Up to this point, I didn't have any real defining moments in the Corps except one and it happened right there in Japan. I took leave and returned to the states to see a friend. I returned to Japan at the conclusion of my leave period via the commercial airlines. I flew from Los Angeles to Tokyo where I was supposed to catch a flight to Okinawa. Often, when flying out of Tokyo, one would have to take a public bus from one airport to another to catch a connecting flight. I was unaware of this.

I only had five dollars in my pocket, which was not enough to get me from Narita International Airport to Haneda Airport. I explained my situation to a guy as I was getting off the plane and he gave me another five bucks stating, "Anything to help a Military guy." Unfortunately, it turned out that the ride from Narita to Haneda was twenty dollars.

I began to panhandle for change outside the airport. I still had time to make my connecting flight, but nobody would give me a second glance. I finally spotted an American and I explained my situation.

"Get away from me you bum!" he said in disgust. I had a full dress blue uniform in my bag. I was ready to die for my country and in an instant I was reduced to a bum on the street. There wasn't anyone I could call. I felt completely helpless. After about an hour, the girl behind the ticket counter came over, gave me a ticket, and put me on the bus. I barely made my flight.

When I arrived in Naha City, Okinawa, I didn't have a ride back to the base and not enough money for a cab. As luck would have it, I spotted a U.S. Navy truck circling in the parking lot.

"Are you Lieutenant so-and-so?" he asked.

"Yes I am; sorry I'm late," I answered trying to perfect the scam.

"No problem sir, hop in," he said happy that he had finally found me. "I'm supposed to take you to Camp Butler?" he asked.

"Actually, you can drop me off at the air station. My car is over there," I said slamming the door.

"You got it, sir," And that's how I got back to base without any money!

CHAPTER 9

Quantico

Quantico, Virginia. It was nothing more than a whistle stop that housed a few bars and restaurants, a couple of barber shops, a drycleaner and one post office. The railroad tracks in the center of town remained from the WWII era when the troops were shuttled to destinations via the rail system. The one main thoroughfare through town led to the marina, which was the only sign other than the post office that Quantico had actually made it to the twentieth century. The town was confined within a ten-foot fence that separated it from the rest of the base.

Quantico is most notably known for the FBI Academy that is neatly tucked away deep in the forests at the opposite end of the base. It also houses a training facility for the DEA, but the heart of the one hundred plus acre government installation is the Marine Corps. It is a major research and development facility for the Corps as well as a maintenance base for HMX-1, the presidential helicopter squadron.

The main street of the base was lined with monstrous brick buildings. These buildings were as old as the base itself, but had had the appropriate face-lifts to disguise their age. The insides hadn't fared so well. The plumbing and ducting were twenty years out of date. It was typical Marine Corps and by that I mean we never acquired anything new. Everything we had was renovated or ten years out of date. The Corps had a saying that a Marine will always adapt and overcome. We stuck to that with everything we did. The Air Force, on the other hand, received the best of everything and it was always brand new. I have to hand it to them; there's a group of folks who know how to get what they want. When they build a base for those guys, they build the fitness center, the officer's club, the commissary, the bowling alley and the movie theaters first. After that, they build the housing and when the money runs out, the government has to give them more because they haven't even begun construction on the airfield! It's brilliant. All the buildings in Quantico looked the same. I couldn't differentiate between the barracks and the chow hall.

The Marine Corps Air Station was the technical name for the airfield that I was assigned to. It was its own base within the base of Quantico complete with its own separate entrance gate. It was a small section of land cast off from the main base and located right on the Potomac River. The barracks had just received an overhaul prior to my arrival, but I had heard the stories of how the Marines had to stay in WWII Quonset huts while the renovation took place.

The chow hall was in shambles. It resembled a rundown truck stop with the exception that the food was well beneath truck stop quality. Most of the guys drove into town to eat. I was shocked that this was the way these guys were treated.

This was supposed to be the best of the best. I had better living arrangements in Okinawa and the chow hall there was top notch.

The airplane hangars were crumbling down. They too were a remnant from WWII that should have been demolished and rebuilt years ago. It would have saved the Marine Corps money to have them torn down. The upkeep wasn't cheap. The doors didn't work, the floors were in dire need of refinishing, the heat didn't work and the whole place was overrun with mice and birds. Understand we were the President's mechanics, we were his personal squadron and this is how we lived. It was embarrassing. Nobody wanted to be there. This wasn't some prized duty station. We were told that we volunteered for this duty. In fact, they made me sign a piece of paper stating just that. The truth was that most of the guys here were here because they had a squeaky-clean record and they were able to pass the background checks to obtain the top-secret clearance that was required. Had I known this, I might have spent a little more time drinking in Pensacola.

I tried to make the best of it. I was excited to be here simply because I would finally get the opportunity to work on a helicopter. Or so I thought. I was floored when I was selected to go to work in what was known as S-4. "S" was short for staffing and most departments of the administration were separated this way. S-1 was generally personnel records, S-2 was training, and S-4 was logistics. It was a fancy term used to describe pushing papers, mowing grass and anything that wasn't helicopter related. It was a ninety day temporary duty that was followed by one month of washing helicopters and moving them in and out of hangars. After that, it was thirty days duty in the mess hall. I was beside myself.

A lot of the guys that I befriended loathed the Corps and HMX-1; the official military designation for the squadron. Clearly they had been down the same road that I was traveling. I tried to keep positive, but the Corps wouldn't let it happen. It had been almost two years since I had finished helicopter school and I hadn't performed a single thread of maintenance. As far as I was concerned, the Corps was in breach of contract!

As more Marines came in after me, I was finally given a chance. I was assigned to work on the night shift maintenance crew. It was short lived though. I was called into the HMFIC's office and he started giving me this salesman's pitch about how I was going to start my air crew training. I laughed.

"What's so funny, Corporal?" he asked.

"Well, Top, nobody wants to do anything with me except put me on detail after detail. I could care less if I work on a helicopter or not. I'm just doing my time," I answered. Top is a nickname given to a guy who's at the top of the rank structure.

"That's not the right attitude to have, Marine!" he fired back. "So you don't want to be aircrew?" he asked.

"No sir," I replied.

"Well what do you think we brought you here for?" he asked angrily.

"Evidently sir, you guys needed someone to mow your grass and cook your food," I replied. He shook his head. He knew there were other things that I could do to benefit this place so he offered me barracks duty or working in the tool room. I took the tool room.

It was nothing more than a hardware store. It was where the mechanics came to get tools to work on the helicopters.

Somebody had to take inventory of all of it to make sure tools weren't left in engine intakes or in the flight controls and that was my new job. It was a cakewalk. I spent more time sleeping and goofing off than I did working.

The job was normally a thirty-day detail for most guys, but the squadron needed someone to run the place full time. It wasn't organized properly and without someone to take a personal interest in it, it wasn't going to get that way.

The tool room also housed something that ultimately turned out to be my saving grace; specialized tools and test equipment, the same as I had babysat in that warehouse in Okinawa. The squadron had its own Individual Materials Readiness List; again a fancy name for a list of equipment needed for war. The squadron was looking for someone that had prior experience. When I made it known that I had worked IMRL in Okinawa, the powers that be had no choice, but to give me the job permanently. This allowed me to have a set schedule. Once again I was working nine to five, which is exactly what I needed to continue my climb up the bodybuilding ladder.

When I arrived at Quantico, I weighed two hundred and fifteen pounds and my training was continuing to improve, but a new duty station presented me with new challenges. I would have to find another source of drugs and locate an acceptable training facility. Quantico's facility wasn't up to my standards. It was located in a WWII airplane hangar and the equipment was old and outdated. I would have to find someplace else to work out.

I found the gym that I was looking for in a rather short amount of time. I just followed the big guys at lunch and struck up conversation. Certainly they would know where the good gyms were and by a "good gym" I mean one that has plenty of drugs floating around.

The place was Champion's Gym. A good-sized gym tucked away in the dying section of Woodbridge, Virginia. The neighborhood was run down. That part of town had been infested by the ever expanding ghetto that was slowly moving south from Washington D.C. The businesses in that area had all moved to the other side of town where a mall had given life to the suburb.

The gym wasn't housed in a sparkling plaza like that which most gyms call home. Gyms in these locations aren't gyms at all. The gym of old has given way to the modern day fitness center. The kickboxing and aerobic crowds have taken over. The dreary dungeons that bodybuilders love don't generate revenue from soccer moms. It's all about the money these days and places like Champion's died when mainstream America decided fitness was cool.

Champion's had an aura about it. I could smell the drugs in the air! There weren't any treadmills or kickboxing here. It was a hard-core crowd that frequented this place. The air had a chalky tint to it from the power lifters coating their hands before the big lift. Slamming the weights down after the completion of a set was the norm. This was the gym your mother warned you about. When the pros were in town, Champion's is where they went. There were drugs in this place; I just needed to find out who was supplying them. I soon made myself right at home.

I knew right off that bodybuilding was going to get more expensive the further I progressed. Gym dues and rising drug costs were just two of the expenses that crunched my wallet. Military pay was hardly enough to cover those costs so I began working part time.

I worked for numerous moving companies and I did everything from warehouse work to truck driving with all of them. When the weekend rolled around and normal people went to museums or visited friends and relatives, I put on jeans and an old sweatshirt and punched the time clock as a common laborer. Our customers were generally companies that were relocating within and around the suburbs of Washington D.C. The pay was good, but the hours were long and the work was back breaking. It was fun, but unfortunately for the clients, we damaged more than we successfully moved.

We once had to clean out the warehouse and some guy had his collectible motorcycles in storage there. We weren't able to start them, but we took them out anyway and rode them down the moving ramps. Of course it was all fun and games until someone rode over the edge of the ramp and dented a very beautiful Triumph. Like the good movers that we were, we just rolled them back to where we found them and covered the damage.

One job that basically sent me with bags packing was a moving job I did in the Georgetown section of the District of Columbia. It was Friday night. The job had started in the late afternoon somewhere in the suburbs and was to end at the top of a three-story walk up in Georgetown. We bullied four big rigs into traffic that was standing still and parked the rigs in the far right lane. As we began to unload, two police cars showed up. The officers started ranting and raving about the mayhem we were causing by blocking traffic. We asked them what they wanted us to do. They had no suggestions so we told them we were going to finish the job with the trucks parked right where they were. They ticketed all four trucks and called a tow truck. The tow truck driver couldn't get in and out of the traffic either so the police decided to continue ticketing the trucks.

At about 10:00 p.m., half the work force walked off the job because they were missing out on their own Friday night activities. Myself and six other guys stayed until early morning to complete the move. Their departure left us severely shorthanded and we ended up trying to move things using one person instead of three. One guy tried moving a safe by bracing himself against the wall. The wall gave way and he went right through it. We received over a thousand dollars in parking tickets that night. The experience gave me a reason to move on.

CHAPTER 10

Marriage

My ex-wife and I met at Champion's Gym. We dated for a very short time before getting married. Our reasons for marriage were all wrong. At the time, we were still learning about each other. I wasn't fully prepared for marriage. It looked good on paper, but the reality of it was, I wasn't responsible enough to make it successful.

As a married couple, we failed to discuss things that really mattered. We never talked about kids or where we wanted to be in five years. We were just two great friends that thought we needed a piece of paper to confirm it.

After we married, I moved off base and we shared a one-bedroom apartment in Dumfries, Virginia. We were like any other newlywed couple in the fact that we didn't have any money. We spent most of our time together at home. She worked two jobs as well. We were trying to pay off a few bills and save for a house.

My steroid habit only served to exacerbate our financial woes. After 1985, steroids became illegal. The federal ban was a mild response to the claim that steroids killed Lyle Alzado, the famous football player. Steroids did not kill Alzado; it was speculation that gave the government a reason. The very first time I purchased anabolic steroids from a mail order company, it cost me thirty five dollars for eight weeks worth. For that same amount now, it was costing me two hundred dollars and up. Even after I located the Mecca of all gyms in Woodbridge, I was still short of a drug connection and the last of what I had brought back from Okinawa was gone. I knew that the Champion's Gym crowd had a source, but it was in short supply due to the government cracking down. People were keeping tight lipped. That's the thing about steroids, if they're in excess, then it's for sale and everyone is willing to help you out, but if it's in short supply, forget it. It's every man for himself.

My job was taking on a routine. The tool room had become the proverbial water cooler where the guys could voice their opinions and complaints. HMX-1 was a place where few wanted to be and many were going to extreme measures in the hopes of getting out. There was a guy who went out to the chin up bars that were positioned between the barracks and the railroad tracks. He waited for the Amtrak passenger train to pass by and when it did, he dropped his shorts to his ankles and began doing chin-ups! It was all in an attempt to get kicked out. I had no intention of getting the boot. I made the deal and I was going to serve out my time. Yes, they had lied to me, but I would out live that contract.

Other guys just gained weight until they didn't fit the proportioned standards. It went on the record as a general discharge, which after six months turned honorable. It was a loophole that afforded a way out without repercussions. Before they would let you go; however, the Marine Corps would drag you along for eight months to a year trying to mold you into that perfect man. At HMX-1, the HMFIC took it upon himself to become the personal trainer of those who were overweight. He made them take part in his fitness regimen in the hopes that they would lose the weight. Progress was checked on a weekly basis. The guys had to endure the forced fitness, but every week at weigh in they would be sure to weigh in heavier than the week before. I helped them achieve that goal by stuffing tools in their pockets before they jumped on the scale. The progress chart showed them overweight by ten pounds one week and twenty the next. Six months later they were being processed for discharge and were well on their way to bigger and better things.

I was adjusting to life in Quantico. I had made a few friends at HMX, but my wife and I never attended anything relating to the Marine Corps. Her attitude was the same as mine. We were ready for me to get out. My evenings were spent in the gym. By the time I got home, we shared an hour or so in front of the TV, and then it was time for bed. We certainly weren't building a quality relationship.

I was spending the weekends on the beach in Ocean City, Maryland. As far as I could tell, I was doing everything I could to further myself in my development. I thought that drugs and working out was what it took. I couldn't have been further from the truth; and on one of those trips to the beach, I met a guy who changed my life as a bodybuilder.

His name was John and he approached me while I was walking on the boardwalk taking in the sights. He introduced himself as a freelance photographer for Muscular Development magazine. I thought he was pulling a scam until he started talking the talk. He told me that he thought I had a future in the sport, but that I really needed help with nutrition and diet. He left the conversation with the infamous "I'll call you." John was true to his word and called as promised.

"Why don't you come up to Laurel and we'll sit down and chat," he said.

I made the drive that opened my eyes to the real sport. He laid it all out in front of me as far as what I needed to do to build quality muscle, i.e. muscle that wasn't covered with fat. He designed a workout and a food program tailored to my needs. He even told me what drugs would work best for me and put me on his list as a client. His list had quite a few local bodybuilders' names on it and they were listed in order as to who got what drugs first. I made the top ten on his list, but his supplier was sporadic at best. I was still going to have to find another source.

John had enlightened me and I followed his teachings word for word. I was now eating eight to ten times a day. I lost my layer of fat by adhering to John's program and my weight went from a fatty two hundred and fifteen pounds to a solid one hundred and ninety. When it was clear to John that I was serious about what I was doing, I moved up a few notches on his list and the drugs came more frequently. It didn't matter though; I had finally made a connection at Champion's.

The birth of the steroid black market forced me to continuously educate myself on what I was taking. I no longer had the luxury of ordering by mail. I had to get my stuff from the dealer that showed up at the gym twice a week. The market proved to be the most dangerous obstacle in bodybuilding. Everybody was out to make a buck and fake drugs were emerging overnight. Thanks to books put out by Daniel Duchaine and others, I became a very well-educated shopper. The first book that I read was The Underground Steroid Handbook and before long I was able to spot a fake from across the room. Guys that were just out to make a buck were buying vials and bottle caps from the local pharmaceutical supply catalog and printing fake labels from their computers. When they were done with their basement productions of testosterone, what you really had was a 10cc bottle of Wesson oil that you paid one hundred and fifty dollars for. The prices went through the roof almost immediately. Guys on the west coast didn't suffer as much as the guys on the east coast since Mexico was, and still is, a big manufacturer of steroids. It was right in their backyard. The big drawback to the Mexican market was that once the pharmacist sold it to you, he'd call customs and give them a picture perfect description of you and they'd be waiting at the border. The pharmacist got a kickback for every guy he turned in. It was just part of the game. Europe was just as difficult to deal with as packages from certain countries were always flagged and probably half of what was shipped was caught by customs. Not until restrictions on foreign medications were eased due to the inability of those with HIV to get the drugs they needed, did bodybuilders manage to exploit the fallacies of the postal system.

Nevertheless, we managed to get things in and out of the shipping port of Baltimore. It was the gold mine for the guys on the east coast. The prices were going out of control and I was on a military salary. The only way to beat that was to put myself right smack in the middle of the action and cut out the middleman. Every time the product touched someone's hands, the price went up fifty dollars. The only way to get around that was to be the guy who got it off the boat. I managed to get it second hand from the guy who got it off the boat and effectively cut my price in half. I was even helping him sell his product to lower the price of what he sold to me. I was supplying most of the users on the Quantico base and half of those in Champion's gym. They knew I was a guy they could trust when it came to steroids. If it was good enough for me, rest assured it was good stuff.

The more I read, the more educated I became. I could now spot a fake by the style of the bottle, the label and label codes or even the place where it was supposedly manufactured. I'm not saying I didn't get taken once in a while. It was nearly impossible not to. The crooks continued to perfect their basement creations and it became increasingly harder to detect a phony. When that happened, I did like everyone else did. I jumped into my car and drove to a gym where nobody knew me and resold it to recoup my loss.

Dealing drugs as a member of "the few and the proud" was easy. I would take orders from the guys while we were eating lunch in the chow hall. I even partnered up with another bodybuilder on base that was getting ready to transfer to California. He already had a customer base that started with a well-known pro. I took orders in Quantico and northern Virginia and called it in to him. I even picked up my packages at the Quantico post office and more than once, opened them in my office in the tool room. The thought of getting caught never crossed my mind. I was consumed with the desire to compete again.

My wife never showed any real concern for the lifestyle that I was living. I passed it off as normal behavior for a bodybuilder and she never questioned it. The reality of it was that steroids had a destructive effect on my marriage. The more drugs I consumed, the less sex drive I had. That caused a lot of dissention between us. Financially, we were barely treading water. That's normal for newlyweds, but had I not been spending four hundred dollars a month on a steroid habit, we probably wouldn't have had the problems we did. She never once told me to stop what I was doing. She never objected so I continued.

After my stint as a furniture mover, I accepted employment at Potomac Mills Mall in Woodbridge as a mall security guard. My wife also had her part time job there. We had hoped that it might allow us to see each other a bit more, but our schedules just didn't mesh.

I guess the first thing that I must tell, and this is probably already in complete alignment with your own suspicions, and that is the fact that mall security is a joke! With that being said, it was still one of the greatest jobs I've ever had. I never took anything seriously. The guys that I worked with were a lot of fun. Every day at work was a comical adventure!

The pay was absolutely horrible for what we were expected to do and was the number one reason we didn't do what we were expected to do. Seven dollars an hour to perform the duties of an unarmed security officer was asking just a little too much. Case in point; I was called on the radio to go to the food court and investigate a report of a man with a gun. I answered the call.

"What do you want me to do?" I asked. "I'm unarmed."

"Just go check it out please," she replied.

"Ok, I'll go," I replied. Of course I never went.

The security force was divided into three shifts that operated around the clock. We also had a dispatch-operations department. The dispatch office had wall-to-wall video screens to display the various camera feeds from around the mall. The cameras covered the hallways, the main thoroughfare of the mall, and the parking lots as well as the food court. The problem was that with only one dispatcher on duty there was no way all the video screens could be watched. The whole system was a waste of money. I'm not even sure the system had recording capabilities. When the dispatcher was at lunch and it was my turn to cover the station, I never watched the screens.

The day shift was comprised of an older generation of retired folks just looking to supplement their retirement checks. It was a known fact that most of the crime events happened at night between the hours of 6:00 and 10:00 p.m. with the exception of Saturday and Sunday. Those two days were crime-filled from open to close.

The midnight shift was made up of another group of retirees. The afternoon shift is where I put my talents to use. My shift was a collection of young military and ex-military guys. We were the workhorses of the security force, the ones who had to chase and tackle the thugs that shoplifted and the ones who wrote all the reports, but at the same time, we were the ones who had the most fun. It was working this job that I met one of the most influential people that I have known in my life.

Doc Brown grew up in Chambersburg, Pennsylvania. He would tell me stories of how he worked in the chicken factory and years after our security days were over, I visited him in that very city. He gave me the grand tour while telling stories about his youth and pointing out the parts of town that had changed since he was a kid.

Doc was placed on midnights, but he always managed to come in early so I could tell him of all the events that had happened on my shift. He would laugh until he had tears in his eyes and then he'd point his finger at me and say, "You really need to keep a journal of this stuff." I took his advice and it was his prompting that led me to write this book.

The mall touted bragging rights as being the largest outlet mall in the country. We covered every inch of it on foot. The building was divided into nine sections, each being defined as a neighborhood. We were assigned a group of neighborhoods to patrol, usually a group of three to four, and we took turns patrolling the parking lot in the small pick-up truck with yellow lights on its top and the word "Security" stenciled on its doors. This was the part of the job I didn't like. It was embarrassing to be seen driving around in this thing. I made it a part of my normal parking lot tour to park the truck in the woods to the rear of the mall. Suburbia hadn't yet sprouted up around the mall's edges and the land was still undeveloped. I spent countless hours sleeping behind the wheel hiding in those trees. On one such occasion, I had parked a little too far over the crest of a hill that lay in front of me and the truck, which only had rear wheel drive, became stuck. I rocked forward then backward, but to no avail. I decided to venture down the slope just enough to gain momentum then veered to one side in the hopes of getting the tires on top of the grass to gain traction. The whole idea fell apart and I ended up rumbling down the hill! As I reached the bottom, I jumped over the ridge that separated the woods from the back road that I was now facing. The truck was out of control. It was sheer luck that I didn't wreck. It took me nearly an hour to find my way back to the mall parking lot. I made it just before shift change. The truck was covered in mud and had tall grass sticking out of the grill when I turned it over to the next guy!

When I patrolled the inside of the mall, I made my share of stops at my wife's place of employment. Working the afternoon shift meant that she would get off work earlier than me and was usually sleeping by the time I got home so this was the only way we could really see each other during the week. On the weekends, I went to the gym bright and early. She followed me out the door heading off to work. It was very rare that we were both home at the same time. I was questioning our reasons for getting married, yet at the same time, I was thankful that I had someone there to support me in the sport of bodybuilding. She was my number one supporter. We continued to look forward to the day when I would be able to leave the Corps. We felt that we would be able to turn our financial situation around and as a result, things in our marriage would improve. By now, we were arguing about finances on a regular basis and it was taking a toll.

CHAPTER 11

Leaving the Corps

As my time in the Corps began its final year, I was training for the title of Mr. D.C. I had enough drugs to get me through the competition and for at least six months thereafter. Gone were the days of "eight weeks on, eight weeks off," when it came to using steroids. It was now a 365-day of the year habit, but was still fairly reasonable at about four hundred dollars a month. I prepared for the show by "dieting down," which is stripping your body of fat and showing the judges striated muscle along with size and symmetry.

I still didn't know what made my body tick and that included my steroid regimen. Certain drugs were for the off competition season and others were for the competition specifically. Bodybuilding is a science and I hadn't quite perfected my approach to all aspects of the sport. On the day of the show, I was on target with my weight, but the muscle striations never really appeared as I had hoped. I did place first in my division, but the competition was sub-par. Nevertheless, it gave me a starting point.

I went back into the gym and trained with fervor. I wasn't anywhere near ready for a national competition, but I now knew what it was going to take to get there. I asked myself what the other guys were doing that I wasn't and the answer kept coming up as "more drugs." I upped my daily dose and my stash dwindled.

My connections were slowly drying up and product was becoming scarce again because the Feds were starting to make busts here and there. After all, they had to make it look like they were really trying to stop the drug flow. Their efforts did nothing more than cause me to step up my own efforts in finding a better source.

While I tried to streamline my life to be more focused on my sport, the Marine Corps attempted to interrupt my efforts with an attempt to send me to Non-Commissioned Officer's School. At this point, bodybuilding ruled me and nothing was going to get in my way of making the pros.

Non-Commissioned Officer's School is essentially just like Boot Camp. It was more marching and running and inspections. We were required to have a complete uniform issue upon reporting for duty but there wasn't a uniform made to fit a guy standing five foot six inches weighing two hundred and twenty five pounds. That meant I would have to have everything tailored to fit and it would cost thousands. I only had three camouflaged uniforms and two dress uniforms to my name and the full issue was a lot more than that.

I've always said that if there's something you want badly enough, then go get it with everything you've got. That logic works in reverse too. I did not want to go to NCO school and I was going to do whatever necessary to not have to go.

So, while engaged in conversation with a friend, who was also a Marine and one that knew the ins and outs of Marine Corps administrative paperwork, my solution came to light. She told me in detail how to alter my training records.

The very next day, I checked out my personnel file. I returned to my office. Sitting down in front of the typewriter, I fed the Official Training Received document over and under the roller. In the column marked "Schools Attended," I listed Non-Commissioned Officer's School, Okinawa, Japan and I even listed fictitious dates. No one ever questioned it and I never attended NCO school. Even though the Corps owned me, they were never going to stand in the way of bodybuilding.

As my exit date from the Corps grew nearer, I stepped up my efforts in searching for a job on the outside that would sustain the lifestyle of a bodybuilder. At that time, I had at least five applications in with five different police departments. The only thing about the job that was appealing was that it was a civil service job and I would be able to use my military time towards retirement. On career day in high school, my results read "Police Officer." I had friends back home that were cops. It seemed like the right fit. How do you stop being a drug dealer and suddenly put yourself on the right side of the law? Fortunately for me, I never had to reconcile the two.

It was a cold Saturday morning and the interviews for the Washington D.C. Metropolitan Police Department were being held at the Martin Luther King Jr. High School in the District of Columbia. I knew the city pretty well from my days as a mover so when I heard the name of the school; I knew it wasn't in the best of neighborhoods. Whenever you hear Martin Luther King as the name of a street or school or building, rest assured it's in the hood. Those that populate the government offices of this country think that by naming something after an African American hero it somehow shows that they care about the plight of the African American people, kind of like throwing them a bone. I consider it a landmark of sorts because it lets me know where to lock my doors and where to drive through the stop signs.

I entered the school amid stares from a couple of hundred people. I was one of about ten white guys applying for the job. In my corner was two hundred and twenty five pounds of muscle and a Marine Corps haircut. Nobody said a word to me. I would probably be walking that beat today had it not been for one old disgruntled cop. I could tell that he was from the old school. He was there for his retirement physical. He looked like he was on the verge of a heart attack. His gut was completely distended and his face was beet red. I was sitting on a bench when he parked his massive belly in my face.

"What are you doing here?" he asked.

"What are you talking about? I'm trying to get a job," I answered.

"You're not that stupid, kid. Look around you. Do you know what's going to happen to you if you get hired? They're going to stick you over on the south side for the first two years and for what? Twenty-five thousand dollars? Wise up kid," he preached. I was making more than that in the Corps. I walked out of the building and headed home.

The last viable option for me was to work in a gym. The money wouldn't be great, but added to my mall paycheck it would allow me to continue my lifestyle. I ventured into a gym in Manassas, Virginia. The manager there had once managed Champion's gym. We knew each other well and he had told me on more than one occasion that if I wanted to work for him, I just had to give him a call. So when he told me that he didn't need me, I felt betrayed. At this point, I didn't have a foreseeable future outside of the Marine Corps. My wife and I talked about my options and we decided that I should extend my enlistment by six months. It was a last resort, but one that I had to use to help get my ducks in line to start a life in the civilian world.

The Marine career planner had gathered my interest in becoming a C-130 cargo plane flight engineer. I felt like I could withstand the Corps if I was at least doing something I wanted to do so I sent in the appropriate paperwork. The lack of work on the outside left me unprepared to leave the safe confines of "three hots and a cot."

By now Champion's Gym had fallen by the wayside. The owner was up to his eyes in debt. It was routine to show up at the front door to find it locked. Finally, the hammer fell and the doors closed for good. I was forced across the street to the not yet opened Olympus Gym, where my reputation was enough to get me in while it was still under construction.

Most of the clientele were former Champion's gym groupies, but the people were becoming more diversified. The treadmill crowds and the aerobic folks had infiltrated the ranks, and the aura of a hard-core gym had died. I stuck it out, but after a while I became the big guy in the gym. That was a title that I didn't want. You have to be the wolf at the bottom of the hill. That's where the inner drive comes from. If the other guys in the gym are bigger than you, that's the push you need to train harder. You have to stay hungry or go home.

When the spring of '91 rolled around, I competed in the East Coast Championships. It was a top-notch caliber competition in which I placed fourth. I just wanted to make the top five. This was the level of competition that would be waiting for me at the National Championships and I now knew that I could compete with them. However, in order to compete at that level, I would have to place first or second at a national qualifying event.

I set my sights on the Armed Forces Championships that were being held in Southern California in the fall of '91. I solicited the Marine Corps to help pay for my travel expenses since there was no way I would be able to afford the trip. They repeatedly told me, "No." This wasn't the first time that I had heard that so I went to the next guy in the chain of command. I pleaded my case and two days before the show, he granted my request. I arrived in top shape and won my division hands down. I was now qualified to compete for professional status. Up to now, competition was on an amateur level, but if I earned my pro ticket, then I would be competing for money.

The following week my wife and I boarded a train headed for New York City. I was going to compete at the New York City Championships. This was the toughest competition I had faced to date. Most of the guys competing were using this show as a tune up for the National Championships. There were even a few notable professionals in the audience. That's how big this show was.

After the preliminary posing, I left the back stage area to take a seat in the auditorium and watch the other competitors. I sat down completely exhausted and the man in front of me turned around to tell me that he thought I looked good and that he had placed me in the top three. It was none other than the 1982 Mr. Olympia, Chris Dickerson. He was a legend. He had competed against all my bodybuilding heroes and had bested them all to win the title. I was floored. I hit the stage that night with more confidence than ever before, but for my efforts I walked away with third place. It didn't matter. I had already qualified for national competition. I was still short of being the best that I could be, but I had the drive and the knowledge of what it would take to get to the professional level. I set my sights on the 1993 Mr. USA.

After a second six-month extension in the Marine Corps, I finally decided that I was going to get out regardless of my job situation. The Corps had filled my head with the prospect of becoming a flight engineer. They dangled the carrot in front of my face for over a year before they flat out refused to give me the position. It was the final insult.

I stepped up my efforts to find a job on the outside. I decided to concentrate my efforts on obtaining my FAA mechanic's license so I would be qualified to work for the airlines. I sent out 125 resumes begging for an airline job.

I continued to deal steroids on the side, but the business in Quantico had slowed. The guys that I had been dealing with were being discharged so my clientele was disappearing. I had to resort to something a little more bold and daring to help with my financial woes. Being in charge of the tool room meant that I was the one in charge of procurement and disposal of said tools. I began ordering tools and selling them to my friends on the outside; everything from vacuums to drills. I also implemented a program that would allow our mechanics to have better quality tools, which would save the squadron millions in the long run. When that program came to fruition, I was told to dispose of the other tools, which I did, right into my own toolbox and what I didn't keep, I sold.

My last hurrah with the Corps probably should have culminated with a court marshal, but they were never able to prove what they had suspected. The phone system on a military base is designed for inter-base use, so most of the phones don't have the capability to dial an outside number. This posed a problem for a guy who was about to be discharged into the world without a job. I needed a way to network from base while I was working. I enlisted the help of an avionics guy (an aircraft electrician) and we tore apart the phone box that was mounted on the back wall of the shop. We dismantled an old rotary dial phone and attached alligator clips to the transmitter and audio wires from the handset. We went one by one from connector to connector inside the phone box until we found a line that would let us dial outside of the base. Once we had that accomplished, we reassembled the phone and modified it so that the alligator clips were hanging out of the back. Now all you had to do to call off base was clip the wires to the connectors that we marked and dial away. I used this procedure to call about job prospects and set up interviews. It was perfect. Of course, I'm not the kind of guy who won't help out the next so I let the other guys in the shop know of the procedure. What I didn't tell them was that somebody somewhere was paying the bill so don't call a number that can be traced back to you. I just figured that they would understand this part. They weren't that smart.

The day the illegal phone got busted was almost my downfall. I was talking to a guy about a job and I heard a click on the line. I immediately hung up, grabbed the specially modified phone and trashed it. I quickly closed the phone box on the wall and sat back down at my desk. No sooner did the door fly open and the HMFIC and another guy stormed in. "Were you just on the phone?" they asked.

"No, Top. Why?" I answered. They started looking at the phone box. They opened it up as if they had a clue what they were looking for. They continued the on-spot investigation and ignored me completely. I just sat there and tried not to look guilty. A few hours later, the HMFIC called me on the carpet. He produced a phone bill for thousands of dollars and asked me, "Do you recognize any of these numbers?"

"No," I replied.

He looked me right in the eye. "I'm going to ask you again, did you call any of these numbers?" I knew there was no way that any of it could be traced back to me. Again I replied, "No."

The other guys didn't fare so well. Those knuckleheads were calling family and friends and the guy on the night shift was calling his girlfriend in Pakistan! Everybody in the squadron knew that he had just returned from embassy duty there. He took the brunt of the blame. I don't know how much he ended up paying.

I had originally signed up for a six-year hitch and ended up doing eight. It all came to a close in January of 1992. I felt like I had wasted a good portion of my young adult life. The greatest problem the Marine Corps faced was itself. It could have been the greatest organization in the world if it only had the proper leadership. Leadership isn't instilled within a person just because they hold a college degree. The Corps needed a program that recognized people for their intelligence and leadership abilities regardless of their rank. I served with guys that were better leaders than the guys who were actually in charge of things. It's no secret that the way you gain rank in the Marines is longevity. Longevity doesn't mean you're smart or that you can lead well, but unfortunately that's how the Corps was managed.

I walked out of the front gate of Quantico the same way I had entered, alone with some papers in my hand. All of my friends were gone. They had all been discharged long before me. I was the last of the Mohicans. The greatest thing the Marine Corps gave me was life-long friends. Today, I have a uniform shirt framed and hanging on my wall simply because it reminds me of all the people I had the pleasure of knowing; people that I'm still in touch with.

CHAPTER 12

American Airlines

The 125 resumes that I had sent out did not generate a lot of interest. I received three calls. Delta Airlines, American Airlines and some fly by night airline called LA Express. The guy in Los Angeles offered me twelve dollars an hour. There was no way I could accept that job. Delta had me out for two interviews and offered me a job, which they reneged on at the last minute, telling me they were going on a hiring freeze. Expecting to be moving, I had already purchased furniture. Now our one bedroom apartment had furniture stacked up in the corner. American called me for an interview, but I didn't get the job due to lack of experience. I was making ends meet with the mall job and sporadic work as an aircraft mechanic in Warrenton, Virginia. I was determined to make it work.

I came to the realization that bodybuilding was going to have to take a back seat to everything else that was going on in my life. Around the same time I left the service, I decided to walk away from the sport. I needed to concentrate on making my marriage work. There wasn't any romance at this point. We were best friends trying to act like a couple. We had separate circles of friends, we never had sit-down meals together, and our work schedules left us communicating via post it notes. Nevertheless, we continued to try to make things work.

American Airlines called me in for a second interview. Thirty five thousand dollars a year plus overtime was a step up from what I was doing so I accepted the offer. The industry was on a down swing, so at that time, airline jobs were hard to come by. Most of the pilots and mechanics were from the Vietnam era so job slots due to attrition were still a few years away. Fortunately for me, however, American was expanding its maintenance at Washington National Airport.

We moved from the Dumfries apartment to a four bedroom, two-car garage house situated on a one-third acre corner lot in an affluent section of Stafford, Virginia. We were now part of mainstream America. It only took nine months to bring order to my life, but I wasn't happy. I still wanted to be a professional bodybuilder.

My return to the sport started out with a remark my wife made. It was a completely innocent comment with no malice behind it, yet it stung me hard. This was the first time I realized that bodybuilding itself, for me, was a sickness. She told me that I was "small." You can't tell a bodybuilder that he is small; it's like telling your boyfriend he has a small penis! Bodybuilding is, for many people, a way to compensate with bodily insecurities. I was always insecure about the way I looked. I don't know what in my inner program drives me to be that way. "Small" was a crushing blow.

That's how quickly life can change. I set out with new determination to be bigger than ever. I began working out in a small fitness room at a recreational center in Dale City, Virginia. It was the perfect little hide-away gym that would allow me to regain my size without suffering ridicule from the guys who knew me when I weighed two hundred and twenty five pounds. I was now a paltry one hundred and eighty. I told the guys that I worked with that I had been a big guy before and that I was going to be that way again. They all laughed. In all honesty, I had my own personal doubts as to whether or not I could pull off a comeback. I had the knowledge, I still had the drive, and now I was making twice the money I was as a serviceman. I could afford the drugs and the ever-increasing intake of food.

I gained most of my weight and size back in the first six months. The guys at work no longer laughed. I was now training for Mr. USA. I still had enough time left on my national qualification to make the show. I was training at Olympus Gym in Seven Corners, Virginia. It was state of the art and the equipment was top notch. I was in with the in crowd of big guys. Drugs were outrageously expensive, but I hadn't figured out another way to get them so I had to pay through the nose like everybody else. I had my own personal dealer who, on occasion, would give me a gym bag full of steroids. The price for the bag was usually in the neighborhood of ten grand. It contained everything a guy would need to get through a competition and for six months after. Three types of testosterone, Halotestin, Anadrol, Sten, Primobolan, Parabolin, Winstrol V, Finaject, Anavar, and the list went on into diuretics and amphetamines. I never took the amphetamines since I had read a book that told how to make your own using caffeine, ephedrine and aspirin. It was just like taking speed. There were times when I didn't hear a sound in the gym except what was going on in my head. The voices, the music and the clanging of the weights didn't register when that stuff was flowing through my veins. It enhanced my ability to push the heavy weights and allowed me to fall deep into a zone.

The gym bag contained it all and I knew for a fact that the stuff was 100% grade A so I marked it up another 100 percent and sold it as fast as I could. The money I made went right back into my own supply. I remember counting out thirteen thousand dollars sitting on my bed before going to sleep. Half of it was mine, but by the end of the next day, I had traded my half for half of what was in the bag. At this point in my life, I was spending at least fifteen hundred dollars a month on steroids and my groceries were costing at least two hundred dollars a week. You don't have to be a math whiz to see how quickly the debt can add up.

The things that I had hoped would turn my marriage into something better only made it more complicated. Buying a house meant a mortgage payment, utility bills, phone bills and credit cards. At one time, we had a combined income of ninety thousand dollars a year, but we had nothing to show for it. We were one paycheck away from the street. I attributed it to the early struggles of being married. Those that have been married can attest to the fact that the first few years are financially tough, but by our third year things weren't getting any better. The house turned out to be a lemon. Our basement flooded two weeks after we moved in. We didn't have the money to fix the damage and legal recourse cost the same as the cost of the repair. We didn't know which way to turn and eventually ended up gutting the basement.

What I thought was going to be my dream job turned out to be a big mistake. The first week introduced me to three supervisors. One stood six feet tall and had a head of gray hair. He had the longest arms of any man that I had ever seen. He slouched in such a way that his arms seemed even longer and made him look like a monkey. We nicknamed him Head because he thought he was the top of the food chain and it rhymed with his real name. We could call him Head to his face and he wouldn't know the difference.

Head had convinced himself that he was the greatest guy to ever work on an airplane and had the audacity to put "jetsrgn" on his license plate. On more than one occasion, a mechanic would prove him wrong in the course of solving a maintenance problem and the only one who wouldn't accept the fact that he was wrong was Head. His great claim to fame was firing a guy on Christmas Eve after he let the guy work his shift! The guy should have been fired long before then, but Head didn't have it in him. The guy was about to complete his six-month probationary period, which meant he was almost a union guy. Head wouldn't be able to fire him if he was union protected so he waited until the last possible day to let him go. He gave another ten guys pink slips the following holiday season. From then on we teased him with the saying, "Ho, ho, ho, someone's got to go!"

The other two supervisors were both named Bob. One Bob worked the day shift and the other worked afternoons. One looked exactly like Ned Flanders from the cartoon The Simpson's. Same hair, same mustache and same body. He even shaved off his mustache at a time that coincided with an episode of the cartoon where Flanders shaved off his mustache. It was eerie to the point of disturbing. I didn't spend much time working directly for him.

The second Bob stood about six feet tall. He was thin and, like Head, he seemed to think he was a gift from God. Rumor had it that he had once been a mechanic, but it was quickly followed with, "he wasn't the smartest one out there." He knew little more than where to fill the engine with oil. He had a nasty habit of sucking his teeth and clicking the heels of his shoes on the tiled floor, but the one thing that really irked me about this guy was that he couldn't pronounce my name! "Feeat, I need you to go do this or that," he'd say. I despised him.

I spent the first few months going to school to learn the basics on the planes that I would be responsible for performing maintenance on. It was a complete waste of money. The lead mechanic wouldn't let any of the new guys work on the aircraft except to add oil to the engines and change the tires and brakes. That was my job for two years.

The first six months on the job were considered a probationary period. The company maintained the right to fire you for any reason during that period, but afterwards you were a made man, a protected union guy and there was no way you could get fired. You could drive a vehicle into the side of a plane and all you had to do was take a drug test to prove you weren't under the influence and then you were awarded three days off with pay to think about your mistake.

My six-month probationary period was miserable. Since the lead mechanic wouldn't let us work on the planes, we were tasked with busywork like cleaning the hangar and the oil storage shed. I worked the midnight shift and hated it. On the morning drive home, I was so tired I would have to pull over into a parking lot and sleep in the car for a few hours.

A typical night while on probation meant sitting in the mechanics' room waiting for someone to come in and say that they needed a guy to change a tire or a brake for them. It wasn't uncommon to spend the first four hours doing just that. When the airplanes were signed off as ready to fly, the union guys went to sleep while the new guys remained in the mechanics' room. Alarm clocks were set for 5:00 a.m. as it was required that everyone be in the room in the event that something mechanically went wrong with a plane while it was parked at the gate. As all the guys crowded into the maintenance room, I stepped into the break room, which was connected by a door. I pulled up a chair and sat in the doorway. When some of the guys left the room, I ventured in and found an open chair. The lead mechanic came out of his office and jumped in my face with a pointed finger. He cursed at me and belittled me in front of everybody stating that I wasn't there when I was supposed to be. I never said a word. It only reaffirmed my conviction that this wasn't the job for me. Not only did horrible management and leadership hamper us, but we also had to deal with the ineptness of the union that represented us. I really can't think of anything good that they did. They lied to us every time the labor contract was up for renegotiation. "We're going to get you guys thirty nine dollars an hour" was the battle cry, but the consolation and reality was, "'Hey guys we got you a dollar-fifty an hour raise.'" The top of the pay scale then was twenty five dollars an hour.

Aircraft mechanics are now, and always will be, under-paid. By the time I left American, I was making thirty dollars an hour. An Escalator mechanic in Washington D.C. working the midnight shift was making forty five dollars an hour. What's the worst thing that can happen if the escalator stops? You might just have to walk up some stairs. An auto mechanic at a reputable dealership can pull down six figures a year and if he screws up fixing your car, what's the worst thing that happens to you? You pull over to the side of the road. On the other hand, what's the worst thing that can happen if that airplane stops midair?

Who's to blame for this overlooked salary differential? The union. Ours had the power to change things, but they chose not to. Plain and simple. The one thing we could count on from them was being laid off at contract time. The only thing that the worker represents to the union is a percentage. When the airline needs cutbacks, the union offers them a percentage of workers to meet that specific cutback quota.

Our biggest problem when it came to the union was that the mechanics didn't have their own separate union like that of the pilot corps. Airline mechanics have an undisputable talent and skill and they should be recognized for it, but as it was, our union encompassed building maintenance, ground support maintenance, and baggage handlers.

When the labor contract is being constructed, the airline tells the union that they will pay a certain dollar amount divided between the various labor groups. If they settle on fifty dollars an hour and there are two groups, say mechanics and baggage handlers, the mechanics will get thirty dollars an hour and the baggage handlers will get twenty. If we had had our own separate union, we would have collected the full fifty dollars. That, coupled with terrible management was one of the root causes of my disgruntled attitude toward that job.

The airline is willing to pay the captain of an airplane upwards of two hundred thousand dollars a year. He should be paid that simply because he is responsible for the lives of all of those aboard the aircraft. He is not being paid to push buttons, which is a tremendous misconception; he is being paid for the responsibility that he assumes and the experience and knowledge that he brings to the table. Now with that in mind, a co-pilot can pull down a low six figure salary yet he assumes no responsibility and he has little experience to offer. The mechanic has just as much responsibility to those same two hundred passengers as the captain. He has to carry a certain amount of experience to be able to maintain and repair the aircraft in accordance with regulations. If they're going to pay the captain for his knowledge and experience, shouldn't they pay the mechanic for the same?

The union had the power to change this, but unfortunately they went under the assumption that greater numbers will keep the airline uppers in check. It's not a novel concept and it worked out for them in the 1930s with the trucking industry and the factory workers, but when the work force is well-diversified between skilled and unskilled labor with the unskilled portion being the majority, the skilled faction becomes part of the lump sum and goes completely overlooked. That was our fate at American. Our union representatives at that time were baggage handlers. They routinely disrupted any efforts for the mechanics to break away and start their own union. They knew that if it were allowed, the airline would cut their jobs and offer them up as part time with lower pay and no benefits. When the contract came up for renewal, this unskilled majority would always put a clause in their contract basically stating that whatever the mechanics get, they get. They knew they needed to ride our coat tails to survive. The union could have, and should have, offered them up for sacrifice. It would have solidified a bond with the mechanics and showed them that their best interests were at the forefront. Using a part time employee for an unskilled labor position is genius and the airline executives would have put the union on a pedestal for the millions of dollars saved. No benefits to pay and no retirement issues to deal with.

After my probationary period, I was like everyone else in the aspect of being able to catch a four-hour nap in the middle of the night. I began to transform myself into a union guy complete with six earrings and a ponytail to the middle of my back. I was comfortable in my surroundings even though I hated the job and I basically set in for the long haul.

Being a member of the union meant that everything was done by seniority. Shift bids to vacation bids and the senior guy had first pick of it all. I got the leftovers, which meant that I had vacation time in January and I didn't get a set shift for a long time. I initially had to work whatever shift needed a warm body due to an absence created by a guy on vacation or sick leave. My schedule was made by afternoon Bob. He routinely scheduled me to work a midnight shift then an afternoon shift the very next day. According to the rules and bylaws of the union contract, this was legal to do, but the company had to pay the worker time and a half for the second shift. The technical term for this was a "quick-turn." I was unaware of the rule until another mechanic told me that what Bob was doing was illegal since I wasn't being paid the time and a half. I filed the union grievance. When Bob received the notice from the union, he called me up to the station manager's office and both of them belittled me for filing the complaint. I wanted what was fair according to the work rules. They pressured me to retract the complaint. Bob lied to the station manager and told him that I had made a deal with him saying that I agreed not to be paid the time and a half. The company was always trying to save a buck.

Away from the job, life was stale. The marriage hadn't improved any. The straight midnight shift was taking its toll on both of us. We weren't even sharing time in front of the

TV anymore. The only way we knew the other person had been home was by the dishes in the sink.

Bodybuilding was the only bright spot in my life. I was getting bigger and had finally figured out a way to eliminate the middleman when it came to steroids. I began taking advantage of the free flying benefit provided by my employer and started traveling to Mexico. It was my place of choice for finding cheap quality drugs. I made many trips across the southern border and more than once completely emptied pharmacies of their steroid supply. What cost five hundred dollars there would cost me five thousand dollars on the market in the states.

Getting through customs was a piece of cake. I had so many ways to disguise my goods that the fear of getting caught never really entered my mind. I'd take the injectable drugs and transfer them into cough medicine bottles and the pills I'd mix in with my regular vitamins. I even taped syringes pre-loaded with testosterone to my waist and waltzed right through Raleigh-Durham's port of entry. I did the same in Miami. I had a few close calls, but in my favor was the fact that customs didn't really know what to look for when it came to steroids. If you showed them a birth control pill, an aspirin, and an Anadrol tablet they wouldn't know which was which. So when the customs agent held up my cough medicine bottle for closer inspection, I didn't sweat it. What worked against me was my size. Mexico was definitely on the custom's list of countries known for illegal importation of steroids and the bigger I got, the more sure I was of getting searched. I finally resorted to hiring a runner. It was usually a skinny guy from the gym who needed a little extra cash and didn't mind spending a few days all expenses paid in Cancun.

It took my personal risk factor out of the equation and still kept my costs down.

Bodybuilding was ruling my world. It consumed the majority of my paycheck. The house payment and the car payment were the last things on my mind. They should have been first, but addiction changes your priorities. I say addiction, but realize that anabolic steroids are not a physical addiction like alcohol or heroine. Steroids don't give you a high, and in fact, you really don't notice any difference until you look in the mirror a few months down the road and see your body taking a new shape. When you take steroids, you become addicted to the way you look when you're on them. I was taking injections five days out of the week. I wasn't a big fan of the pills so I only took them when I felt it was truly necessary. Pills are harder on your system than injectables, as they have to travel through your digestive tract and internal organs. This process actually lessened the beneficial effects. Injecting the drugs, on the other hand, allowed the drugs to go right into the muscle and the bloodstream, which made them more easily used by the body without the chance of being destroyed by the organs.

Eating had become a full time job. It had become a chore and it was something I had to force myself to do at times. People don't really understand how much food a person must consume to force the body to grow so let me describe how a Saturday would go in my life as a bodybuilder. I would get up at 6:00 a.m. and make French toast, using a whole loaf of bread, and cram it down my throat. I'd call my training partner to see if he was up and we would make arrangements to meet at the gym or I would pick him up on my way. I would start the rice cooker and at the same time make six sandwiches of various types. By now, it was 7:30 a.m. and I was downing some fruit and a bowl of oatmeal. I would throw the sandwiches in my bag and head out the door at about 8:00 a.m. The drive to the gym was forty-five minutes. The workout would last an hour and a half, which put me walking out of the gym at or around 11:00 a.m. I'd walk over to my car and eat a sandwich. My partner and I would walk across the parking lot to a local restaurant. I'd eat a one-third pound steak sandwich before making the drive home and on the way home I'd manage to make another sandwich disappear. On occasion, I'd hit McDonald's up for six hamburgers and have them all eaten by the time I reached home. Once I got to the house, I'd sit down to chicken, rice and broccoli. I ate that at least two more times during the day and I'd finish the sandwiches in between. My last meal would go down at 10:00 p.m. The lunch box that I took to work was a small cooler. I regularly packed it to the top and finished it by the end of my shift.

My body continued to grow at such a fast rate that my joints couldn't keep up. I began experiencing pain in my right knee and decided to see an orthopedic surgeon. The diagnosis was torn cartilage. All my hopes and dreams were swirling into the drain and that loud accompanying sucking sound was playing like a broken record in the back of my head. I had never seen this in my crystal ball. The doctor assured me that with proper rehab, I would be back at it in a reasonable amount of time. I elected to have the surgery and miss the Mr. USA.

CHAPTER 13

Lay Off

After the surgery, I did exactly what the doctor prescribed and the knee came back to form just like he said. He gave me a strong word of caution though, stating that if I continued to squat the heavy iron both knees would be at risk. I had ignored every word of caution when it came to taking steroids, GHB (Gamma-Hydroxybutyric Acid) and growth hormone. I had made a speed concoction that effectively blocked out life for an hour and a half at a time. I had shot chemicals in my body that most people didn't know existed. So when the doctor stood there and offered me advice, I thought to myself, "Hey I'm still standing, I'm invincible." I continued to pound the weights and my five foot six frame was now supporting two hundred and thirty five pounds of meat.

Things in the bodybuilding world were really looking positive until American Airlines joined the rest of the industry and decided to lay off part of its workforce. I look back now and realize that it was the best thing to ever happen to me while I was employed there. That sounds a bit preposterous, but it forced me to start thinking about another career. Yes it put me in a serious financial bind, one that took me years to recover from, but it made me come to grips with the fact that this job wouldn't be around when it came time to retire. I pulled out my earrings and cut my hair and started looking for a job.

When I had the actual pink slip in my hand, I loaded my tools into my car and drove home thinking about my options for the near future. I was kicking myself for taking this job to begin with. Not only had I lost my job, albeit temporarily since it was just a lay off, but now my drug connection had been severed. There was no way that I would be able to continue to fly to Mexico if I was on lay off status.

The next few months proved to be a very trying time in my life. I joined the folks at the unemployment line. There is nothing more defeating in life than to have to present yourself to the public welfare system to get a paycheck. The folks at that office are some of the most ill-bred, uncivil and ungracious people I've ever met.

Though they had been happy to accept our monthly dues, now that we were on a forced sabbatical, the union completely abandoned us. My unemployment entitled me to two hundred and eight dollars a week. That didn't even cover my grocery bill. I received my first check after the mandatory two week waiting period. In the mean time, I was out looking for work every single day.

My unemployment checks were coming in sporadically because American Airlines had reported to the state of Virginia that I had received vacation and sick leave pay. If you receive any income other than your unemployment, you have to report it and then it's deducted from your unemployment benefits. Now, I hadn't received either, but the unemployment checks stopped coming for two weeks. At this point, I was dealing steroids to put food on the table.

I received two more checks from the state before they abruptly stopped again. When I went to the office to find out why, they informed me that American had reported for a second time that I had received vacation and sick leave pay. I tried to explain that it was a mistake. When they failed to grasp this, I became angry and frustrated and quit filing the paperwork.

The following week I landed a job working as an equipment technician at the National Institutes of Health, (NIH). The job was supposed to pay thirty thousand dollars a year, but ended up being twenty seven thousand. It was a thirteen thousand dollar pay cut from the airline, but what was I going to do? I needed the job. It was a fun job that gave me freedom and independence. The work was easy. I rarely saw my boss except on Friday when he took me out to lunch and gave me my check. I had free reign of NIH and I dictated my own work schedule as well. I had a certain amount of work that had to be completed by the end of the month, which meant that if I finished it by the twenty third; I was basically work-free until the first. The company provided the tools too. The only drawback was the commute to and from. It took me an hour each way.

NIH is set up like a college campus. It is a bunch of buildings sitting on forty acres of property. It also has its own hospital. I divided my time between the research laboratories and the hospital repairing and installing equipment. One day while I was working in the labs, I stumbled across a catalog. It was a catalog for drugs similar to the one where I had purchased my first steroid order in 1985. My mouth watered! Laboratory grade cocaine, amphetamines, heroine, it was all there, but my interest wasn't in narcotics. I continued to surf the pages and found what I was looking for. Growth hormone; better known as GH in the bodybuilding world, and worth its weight in gold. In combination with steroids there is nothing better in the world for building muscle. I took the catalog and quickly devised a scheme to acquire the GH.

I called the number listed in the catalog. "Hi my name is Doctor Fett at the National Cancer Institute. I'm currently working on a project using growth hormone and I've run out. I have a deadline to meet by Friday and I'm wondering if I can put this order on my personal credit card. I'll deal with the red tape of getting reimbursed on my end, but I really need it," I stated.

"No problem, Doctor Fett, how much do you need and where should we ship it?" the voice on the phone responded. Unbelievable. I whipped out my credit card and charged it to its limit right there on the spot. Seven thousand dollars worth was delivered to me via Federal Express the very next day at an abandoned office at the National Cancer Institute. The street value was in excess of fifty thousand dollars. I ended up making enough to pay off the credit card and had plenty of cash to spare.

I also scored a steroid connection in one of the many pharmacies located in the hospital. I met a girl there that told me she had a friend in the pharmacy who could get me anything I wanted. She was referring to narcotics and was a little puzzled when I gave her a list of the drugs that I was looking for. She said she would check on it and within a week, her guy was getting me what I had requested.

At this point in time, my steroid problems had been solved. I had my sights set on national level competition, but with the time off after my discharge from the service and the time it took to rehab my knee, my qualification to compete at that level had expired. The qualification is only good for two years. Now I faced the reality of having to compete at a national qualifier to re-qualify. I set out with the same determination that I did with everything and found myself looking the best I ever had in my bodybuilding career. The competition preparation process went almost textbook perfect. I figured that I was about two years from being a contender for my professional ticket. I re-qualified for national level competition in the fall of '94 by winning my class at a show in Virginia. I was confident that I would be able to make a respectable showing at the '95 Mr. USA and I set out to do just that.

By now, my joints were hurting on a daily basis. My elbows hurt so bad that many nights I would wake up and cry from the pain. I periodically had lactations from my nipples. It's a side effect that bodybuilders don't talk about. Some guys get gynocomastia. It's a condition where the fatty tissue in the pectoral muscle swells around the nipple. I never suffered from that, but to have lactating nipples as a guy was detrimental to my psyche. At one point, I ended up in the hospital with purple and green ankles that were severely swollen from gaining weight at such a rapid rate. I gained twenty five pounds in two weeks immediately following a competition. That's a little on the unhealthy side. All of this was culminating as my national debut was fast approaching. I swore to myself that after the show, I would take time off to let my body recuperate.

Even though my drug dealing was bringing in a little extra cash, more often than not, I used it to buy more drugs for my own stockpile. This led me to make up the pay difference between NIH and American by taking on a part time job. I was hired as a cook at a chain restaurant in Springfield, Virginia. Though it helped with the bills, it pushed my marriage over the edge. Now I was away from home for at least twelve hours at a time. There were times when I was so tired I didn't even go to the house at the end of the day. It was now official; we were nothing more than roommates. Divorce was imminent, but neither of us could afford to live on our own. The only way we could save any money to make the jump to being single was to stop paying the mortgage. We did that for three months and then the house was up for sale.

We sold it cheap due to the condition of the basement. We walked out of the realtor's office after closing on the deal and until we started our divorce a year and a half later, there wasn't any contact between us. We were angry at each other for the way things turned out. I was embittered with myself for letting the relationship linger for as long as it did.

On top of our separation and the loss of our house, bodybuilding was suddenly dealt another crushing blow. I wish I could tell you that I competed at the Mr. USA and made the bodybuilding world take notice. I wish I could tell you that I took the time to heal my body, but had any of that happened, I wouldn't be writing this from inside a tin can at 37,000 feet! The fact of the matter was that my left knee was now experiencing the same pain that my right knee had. I never thought that I would suffer an injury that would jeopardize my bodybuilding career. I didn't take part in any other physical activities, fearful of the repercussions if something went wrong. I didn't ski or play recreational sports. I didn't drink or party. Bodybuilding isn't just a sport; it's a lifestyle. Your daily routine affects your ability to grow. It affects whether or not you're going to have a good workout or a bad one. Physically and mentally I had sacrificed so much to reach my goal and now my body was falling apart. I had no choice, but to have the knee surgery. Unfortunately again, it was five months out from the Mr. USA so I had to scrap the show once more. I was completely distraught. I was in the best shape of my life now weighing two hundred and fifty pounds and I wouldn't be able to compete.

After the surgery, I went into a depression. Not only was my body falling apart, but the divorce was complicating my life as well. On top of that my car died and I was forced to buy a vehicle at a time when I was still trying to financially recover from being laid off. I tried to cope with each problem individually, but the task was daunting. There were times when I just completely lost control. The day I traded my car in, I was so angry that I took a baseball bat and started beating on it right there in the car lot. The salesman came running out.

"If that's your trade in sir, you'll have to stop that!" he screamed.

I continued to work out and baby-step the rehab on my left knee, but even with a slow therapeutic approach, the pain never really went away. It became tolerable, but the workouts were suffering tremendously. I eventually became so frustrated that I stopped altogether. I was tired of the needles and pills and the aches and pains. I was tired of eating. I was tired of always being in debt. I had never planned for life after bodybuilding, life after the roar of the crowd stopped. Now I would have to face the music and I would have to face it on my own.

I lay awake at night remembering the powerful feeling of capturing the cheers of a couple thousand people. It was the most exhilarating experience. Now I was terrified of being a normal guy. Just as I had learned what it took to become a massive piece of meat, I would now have to learn what it was to be normal. The sport had driven me to sickness, not just because I was deathly afraid to be one hundred and seventy five pounds, but because I had developed an eating disorder. I had survived all the drugs, but succumbed to the power of food. Medically termed ED-BT, which is short for Eating Disorder, Bodybuilder Type; psychiatrists define it as reverse anorexia or the coined phrase "bigorexia." It is a form of obsessive-compulsive behavior. It comes from an obsessive need to be certain that all meals contain the right amount of proteins and carbohydrates and in the correct caloric intake needed to maintain or grow the specific physique that you are trying to achieve. The medical world says that if you spend more than five hours a day thinking that your body is underdeveloped, then you may suffer from this affliction. I had all the telltale signs. I still fight it though not with the same nervous intensity that I used to.

When it was all said and done, I was roughly twenty thousand dollars in debt, divorced and living in a two-bedroom apartment. I had been possessed with the lifestyle of bodybuilding for over ten years. I had a shelf full of trophies, two bum knees, and a collage of pictures that preserved all my bodybuilding heroes. My sister made it especially for me when she was in second grade. I used to look at it and dream about being one of those guys, and as I removed it from my wall, I felt like I was letting go of the biggest thing in my life. It was time to retire. I still have that collage and now and then I take it out as a reminder of where it all started and where it all ended.

The last order of growth hormone was still sitting in my refrigerator. I was unable to sell it because most of the guys that I dealt with couldn't afford it. I had bought a specific amount because a friend of mine said he had the money and wanted it, but as fate would have it, he didn't come up with the cash. I ended up adding another seven thousand dollars of debt to my financial nightmare. I finally had to throw it away.

I also had to dispose of my second refrigerator. That's how much food I consumed. I needed a second one to hold my groceries. I sent a care package that contained the last of my steroid collection to a close friend. When I put the postage on the box, I suddenly felt absolved from the sport. We parted on good terms, but from that day forward, I've always felt a little bit like a failure. I could have accepted leaving bodybuilding if I had competed at the national level and been beaten, but that wasn't the case. I was defeated because my body couldn't hold up and that's a hard pill to swallow.

CHAPTER 14

Back to Work

I was called back to work in October of '95. Though I despised the job, I was thankful to be back. I continued to work at the restaurant as well. I figured if I put my nose to the grind, the income from both jobs would get me out of debt. I was now working 16 hours a day.

I had no life outside of my two jobs. Everything I owned was still wrapped up in boxes and being stored in one of the two bedrooms in my apartment. My bed filled the other room, but I never slept in it again after my wife and I separated. I had a television that was ten years old and a lazy boy chair that sat in the living room next to a loveseat. The chair became my bed as I took up the habit of sleeping with the television on. On occasion, I would pull out the sofa bed from under the cushions of the loveseat.

My apartment was located in a severely deteriorated section of Woodbridge. To add insult to injury, every now and then my car was broken into or vandalized. I figured that if I accomplished the goal of getting out of debt, my world would change.

I really enjoyed working at the restaurant. I mastered the grill. It got busy at times, but I was able to keep the food rolling out of the window. After the dinner rush, I spent about an hour or so cleaning up the kitchen and then it was out the door. It was another no-brainer job that offered easy money. Though I started working at the restaurant on the weekends, I eventually found myself there five days a week. The pay was eight dollars an hour and the managers were idiots. So why did I stay there for two years? Two reasons; extra income, and it was the most fun I've ever had collecting a paycheck.

There were only four adults that worked in the kitchen other than management. The rest of the work force was comprised of high school teenagers and a few twenty something flunkies. Amazingly, we all shared one thing in common and that was we just didn't care about anything concerning the restaurant. The rules were simple. Don't eat anything you haven't paid for and when business is slow; look busy. We just didn't have the ability to adhere to the simplicity of those guidelines. We ate every minute we were there and didn't pay for any of it! I can honestly say that my grocery bill at home diminished by half after my employment. We, meaning everyone from the servers to the cooks to the dishwashers, took up the hobby of stealing the food as soon as it rolled down the ramp of the delivery truck. It was routine for the dishwashers to swipe a case of steaks, toss it in the garbage can as if they were taking out the trash, then cart it out to the dumpster behind the building. It would be sitting behind the dumpster at quitting time along with hamburgers, chicken breasts, French fries and even desserts. We had so much food sitting behind the dumpster we could have started another restaurant.

Working behind the grill allowed me the golden opportunity to cook for my friends and myself. It was not unusual for me to eat two complete dinners before the end of the dinner rush. I just threw it on the grill with the rest of the food. Nobody knew the difference. When it wasn't busy, we spent time inside the cooler escaping the heat and we ate everything in there as well. It's no wonder we had at least five management changes while I was there; the numbers at the end of the month never came out right!

Now I've told many of my closest friends what to and what not to do when it comes to sending food back to the cook. There is a proper way to do it and I highly recommend you follow it. The destiny of your returned food is in direct proportion with the attitude you displayed when returning it. "This steak isn't quite done, can you put it back on the grill for a few minutes?" is the correct way to do it. Say something like, "I asked for medium and this is not medium!" and you are just about guaranteed to receive a "floor steak" in return.

We went to great lengths to outdo each other in viciously abusing a customer's food. To this day, I WILL NOT send my food back. If my steak shows up well done and I asked for rare, too bad, I'll eat it with a smile on my face!

There were quite a few other cooks during my tenure there and it always seemed like just as I was getting to be good friends with one they would quit and move on. My companions on the grill were Todd and Blaine. Todd held the dubious honor of being the only non-Hispanic to work the dishwasher. I had to approach the manager and tell him to put Todd on the grill because I needed another cook. I felt sorry for him being the only one in dishwashing that spoke English.

Both Todd and Blaine were still in high school and both were delinquent to the core! I walked into the kitchen one afternoon prior to my shift and found these two characters playing hockey with a piece of chicken. They looked like two cats that had swallowed canaries.

"Who is that for?" I inquired.

"The manager!" they replied in unison. "He told us that we were going to cook his dinner. That lazy bum could have done it himself. Now he'll pay the price!" they continued.

"That's my boys!" I said smiling and giving them my thumbs up. An hour later the manager came out to tell them that his chicken was the best he ever had.

I desperately tried to get afternoon Bob to come in for dinner. I yearned for the opportunity to get revenge for the way he treated me, but I had told the guys there about the crazy things we did so Bob was well aware. He flat out refused to come to the restaurant even after I offered to pay!

"I don't trust you, Feeat," he said rebuking my offer.

The restaurant was an outlet for everything that was wrong in my life. Although the opportunity to express my childish behavior was a major reason for me to stay, so were the people that I worked with. I made some lifelong friends during my stay there. A few of them I am still in touch with today like Todd and some of the girls from the wait staff. The people are what made the memories and the laughter at a time in my life when I needed it most.

One of those people was the guy in charge of cooking prep. He was a middle-aged African-American named Elwood Scott. We all called him Scotty. He was the one who kept me steadily supplied with food so I could work my magic on the grill. He was also one of the guys who kept me laughing. He reminded me of Fred Sanford especially when he walked. He had two beat up knees from his days of playing football that caused him to shuffle his feet with a left and right jog of his shoulders. Even though it looked like it was painful for him, it always seemed to me a graceful movement reminiscent of his days on the field.

"Hey now! There he is!" Scotty hollered out with a smile that stretched from ear to ear as I walked through the kitchen at the start of my shift. We'd high five or pound fists as we passed.

"How are things looking, Scotty?" I asked.

"It's just about ready," he assured me.

You see, the guy on the grill can't do anything without the guy in kitchen preparation. He's the backbone of the whole operation. As I returned from the break room decked out in my green apron and ridiculous paper hat, I walked over to him and asked, "You hungry?"

"What do you got?" he answered.

"What do you want?" I countered.

He laughed and replied, "Whatever you're fixing!"

Scotty and I had dinner on the house every day we worked together. I would fix his dinner and put the plate in an empty pot then holler out, "Scotty I need more ribs!" He would come from around the corner and I would hand him the pot. I think he actually thought I needed ribs, but when he removed the lid to see his dinner, he would smile that wonderful smile and his eyes would light up. He shook his head from side to side and said, "My man, mmm."

Many nights after work, I would drive Scotty home. Usually when it was too cold or raining and always when his knees hurt. I loved those nights. When we arrived at his place, if we had any food from the restaurant, we cooked it up, if not, then we just sat on the front steps and talked. Scotty and I had more in common than you would think. I was sitting in the presence of greatness. Here was a man that missed his shot at pro football by about the same distance I missed pro bodybuilding.

"Man you should have seen me! They couldn't catch me!" he bragged. He stood up and juked his shoulders left then right. "Just like that, I'd leave them right where they stood!" he continued. I had visions of the great Floyd Little tearing up the middle of the line. At that moment, he and Scotty were one in the same.

"Do you miss bodybuilding?" he asked.

"Every day of my life," I replied. The silence engulfed us, both of us reminiscing in our own minds of the days when we were kings.

"Did you see that?" I asked referring to the shooting star that streaked across the sky. He never heard my question still lost in yet one more record-breaking football game.

Scotty had played on one of the All-Delco (short for Delaware County in Pennsylvania) football teams in the late '60s. He played with guys like Billy "White Shoes" Johnson, John Cappelletti, and Ed O'Neil, all of them eventually ending up in the pros. All, but Scotty.

He was a superstar quarterback in high school and after graduation moved on to hone his skills at McPherson College in Wichita, Kansas where he played for two years. For reasons unknown to me, he left college after his second year. By the time he returned to the game, his window of opportunity was quickly closing. He did get a tryout with the Kansas City Chiefs, but was cut in training camp. He went on to play semi-pro ball with the Tulsa Knights in the early '70s, but when the dream didn't pan out, he joined the Navy.

When we met, he was struggling to earn enough money to pay the bills just like the rest of us. He told me that his high school was going to induct him into their sports hall of fame and he wasn't sure if he was going to be able to make it back for the ceremony. So I put Scotty on an American Airlines flight headed home.

"How do I look?" he asked straightening his tie.

"You're going to knock them dead!" I told him.

I watched the plane depart with greatness aboard.

When he returned, he hit me with that smile and I knew right then that for a moment in time he had been back on the field.

Scotty and I kept in touch after I left the restaurant and I stopped in to see him every now and then if for nothing more than to give him a ride home. I even called him once in a while to check on him. I remember the last phone call we shared. He was trying to go home again and I told him all he had to do was say when.

Scotty passed away in the late '90s. His family called and invited me to the service.

By now, I was working ten-hour shifts with four days on three days off. In addition to the two jobs I was working, I was also going to school at the Brazilian Cultural Arts Institute to learn Portuguese. It was another activity that kept me from dwelling on my current situation. I soon moved over to another local restaurant to continue earning a part time income. The pay was better, the stress was less, and the management was good. I was still in financial straits, but once again the people I worked with made the job worth it.

The job with American became very predictable and routine. Punch the clock at ten and go to sleep at one. There were many nights when I left work to go to an afterhour's party with the folks from the restaurant. Nobody would miss me. They wouldn't be awake until five anyway. I'd show up at the party in my mechanic uniform and everybody would laugh.

"That's right, it's a union job!" I'd tell them.

There were other times when I'd just go home. The drive was only thirty minutes.

Along with being mundane, the airline job always made me feel like an outsider. I could count on one hand the number of guys that I would call friends. We routinely had weeks where we would follow the union rules to the script in retaliation to something that management did. I always felt that we stopped the protest short of accomplishing anything. Two days of protesting something is hardly a protest, but that's how it was with some of these guys. They didn't have the determination to see it through. We were union guys and we had the ability to run that operation to our liking, but we lacked unity and nerve.

My attitude didn't earn me any more friends. I recall a time when the company attempted to remove the four days on three days off schedule and implement a normal five-day workweek. Management called everybody into the office. Myself and two other guys refused to go. We waited outside. When the meeting was over, the guys had buckled to management's request and our protest was over one day after it had started. One of the guys approached me later that night trying to explain why they did what they did. I was furious.

"Look, you're not going to be here for the rest of your career, I am. This is all I've got. You're already planning on bigger and better things, we all know that," he stated.

"If you back off, you're never going to get what you want!" I told him.

From that day on, I was the outsider. When the other guys got the invites to barbeques and weddings, I was left out in the cold. He was right when he said that I wasn't going to be there forever. The company didn't care about its employees and the union didn't care about its members. There was no way that I was going to hang around for the long term.

It took me two years of working two jobs fourteen hours a day to finally pay down twenty thousand dollars of debt to a mere two thousand. Unfortunately, I was putting money into a pathetic 401k program so my retirement funds weren't adding up. As it was, the only funds in the program that we had access to were funds that were run by AMR; the parent company of American Airlines. If you invested one thousand dollars in January, by the end of the year you still had one thousand dollars. It was wretched.

It was clear to me at this point that my life was in dire need of an overhaul. One night, while I was engaged in conversation with a pilot, he told me how much he loved his job. I was so jealous. I couldn't imagine what that was like because up to this point in time, I loathed my job, my life, and my outlook for the future.

CHAPTER 15

Making Changes

To make a change in your life you need the desire to do it and the commitment to see it through. I had the desire to change my life. Every night that I went to work fueled it further. I continued to tolerate the mediocre management at American. Afternoon Bob became the focal point of my anger as he found his way onto the midnight shift after Head retired. He did things to purposely get under my skin in the hopes of me retaliating to the extent that he would have reason to fire me.

One evening I had laid my nightly paperwork in front of my locker on top of some newspapers. He picked up the stack of papers and put them in his office. Upon returning to my locker and noticing the papers gone, I ran out of the room in search of the night cleaner who I thought may have picked them up in error. I sifted through numerous bags of garbage and wasted hours looking for the missing papers before he finally confessed to having them in his possession.

He said he was trying to teach me a lesson. Suddenly, I was being treated like a ten-year-old kid. I was one step away from battering this man with the hammer from my toolbox. In fact, the lead mechanic asked me to go home early because he knew I was going to do something that I would regret. Afternoon Bob reaffirmed my decision to leave American. My biggest problem in doing that was money. I had bills to pay and I had no intention of defaulting on any of them. My finances had to be in some sort of order for me to be able to walk away. I now knew what career I wanted to pursue and that was flying.

Some friends in the Marine Corps first introduced me to flying in the early '90s. We regularly flew to the beach in Ocean City, Maryland in a four seat Cessna airplane. Almost immediately I enrolled in a ground school course to learn the basics of flying. Ground school is where you learn how to navigate, how the instruments work, and the rules and regulations. Like everything in this world, flying costs money and in the early '90s, I didn't have any. I managed to get about three-quarters of the way through the private pilot course before calling it quits. Six years later I still had the desire to be a pilot so I finally made the decision to give it another try. I was now divorced, bodybuilding was a fading memory and I had finally made my way out from under my immense debt. There was nothing preventing me from pursuing a pilot's license and during a phone conversation with one of the guys who had introduced me to flying, the decision was made.

"Are you still flying?" he asked. He was no longer a private pilot on the weekend. He was a warrant officer in the United States Army flying helicopters.

"No I kind of had to give it up," I replied.

"Well get out here to Arizona and we'll get you back in the sky," he said.

I took a week off from work and headed out to the desert. He sat down with me and refreshed my memory of the things I had learned in the ground school. We went over navigation at length since that was my greatest weakness. We then ventured out into the sky in a rented four seat Cessna. He flew the plane out over the desert then gave me the controls and told me to take us home. I had no idea where we were so he pulled out the map and showed me how to find myself and locate landmarks. More importantly, he taught me how to remain calm. I found our way home and when I returned to Virginia, I enrolled in flight school again.

There are different types of licenses in aviation depending on what type of flying you want to do. The first is a private pilot's license which allows you to fly on a sunny day. The next in line would be the instrument license. It allows you to fly in bad weather and in the clouds. Then there is the commercial pilot's license, which allows you to fly in bad weather and get paid to do it and finally, the coup de gras, the doctorate of flying; the airline transport pilot's license. You'll need this if you have aspirations of flying for the airlines. My goal upon re-enrollment was to obtain every one of them.

The cost to get a commercial pilot's license at that time was between thirty thousand and forty thousand dollars. It would cost the same if I had gone to a four-year college to obtain it or the flight school at the local airport. I chose the local airport, which happened to be the Warrenton-Fauquier County Airport in Warrenton, Virginia. I tried to finance the training with a bank loan, but every one of them told me that I made too much money for that type of loan. What is "too much money?" I was making seventy five thousand dollars a year with American Airlines, but I certainly didn't call that "too much money." So I put it on my credit cards. I was willing to go thirty five thousand dollars in the hole for my education and a new career so while I was working the midnight shift and in between the days that I worked at the restaurant, I was learning how to fly. It took me about two months to finish what I had previously accomplished in pursuit of my private pilot's license and in the winter of '99 I held that license in my hand. I continued my training and spent the next six months working to obtain my instrument license. I stumbled during this portion of the training, but I never gave up. I routinely asked the pilots at American for help and they routinely shrugged me off. It only fueled the fire inside of me. I finally prevailed and in the spring of 2000 I was an instrument pilot.

My first plunge into the skies as a solo instrument pilot almost ended in disaster. I had rented a plane and had plotted a course to New Jersey. The weather was perfect for a new instrument pilot. I departed from the airport in Warrenton a bit nervous, but definitely up for the challenge. I penetrated the clouds with confidence under instructions from Air Traffic Control. The airplane was purring like a kitten. ATC came over the radio: "You're cleared to such and such intersection." This was going to be a piece of cake. I had my handheld GPS sitting in the seat next to me so I leaned over and started pushing buttons. Unbeknownst to me, I turned the airplane. Not only did I turn it; I actually pointed the nose slightly down. The only indication I had that anything was amiss was the sound of wind rushing outside the window. I looked up from the GPS to find that the airplane was turned thirty degrees to the right and descending at fifteen hundred feet per minute! I grabbed the yoke and leveled the wings. I pulled the power back to idle as my speed was just outside the red line. ATC came across the radio in a calm yet concerned voice. "Uh aircraft so and so we show you 30 degrees off course and descending. Is everything ok?" At this point, I was in dire panic.

"No I'm not ok!" I replied frantically. "I'm a new instrument pilot and I'm disoriented!"

"Ok," he replied. "Is the aircraft level?" he asked.

"Yes sir," I answered. "Hold that heading and climb to niner thousand," he continued. "You should break out of the tops at about eight thousand five hundred." He was right on the number. I shot out into the blue sky at that exact altitude. My hands were shaking so bad that I couldn't even turn the radio knobs. I continued the flight to New Jersey on top of the clouds and flew back home below the overcast. My confidence was gone and I had to hire a flight instructor to fly with me again to shake off the heebee jeebies.

The debt was again piling up, but in my mind it was justified. I relished the thought of leaving American. I took a few weeks of vacation and headed to Florida to get my multi-engine license. As the name indicates, this would allow me to fly planes with more than one engine. When you are coming up through the ranks, multi-engine flight hours are worth their weight in gold, but they are also twice the cost. I spent roughly five thousand dollars for that trip to Florida, but it included an apartment plus fifty hours of flight time in addition to the multi-engine license. I returned to Virginia with only the commercial license standing in my way. There's a commercial license for single engine planes and then there's one for multi-engine planes. Most guys get both, but the only purpose for having a single engine commercial license is so that you can become a paid flight instructor. I had no intention of becoming a flight instructor as I barely had confidence in my own newfound abilities as a pilot. I didn't want to take the chance of having someone put me in a situation that neither one of us could get out of. I went straight into the multi-engine commercial training and within a month I had passed all the tests. I was now a commercial pilot with 300 hours of total flight time. That and two bits will get you a cup of coffee! That's one of the big fallacies of aviation. Having a license without substantial flight hours means nothing. The minimum amount of flight time needed to fly at a major airline is about 5000 hours. I had already spent thirty five thousand dollars and had accumulated only 300 hours. I could see that to survive on this side of aviation's fence I would need a big break. I kept building my flight time, courtesy of bank plastic. The debt grew larger and I was well past the point where I had told myself that I would no longer charge the flying.

I was gazing at the three credit card statements just before I decided to dust off the fishing poles and head out to the Occoquan Reservoir. It was a ten-minute walk from my run-down rented townhouse. How in the world did the other guys make it in this industry without going broke? Guys like me don't often make it. The pilot corps of aviation was never meant for blue-collar folk.

On occasion, I reflected back on bodybuilding and how much I missed it. Every now and again I was reminded of what could have been by those around me. One of my flight instructors turned to me during one of our flights together.

"Didn't I see you on ESPN the other night?" he asked.

I confirmed his suspicions and told him that it was a rebroadcast of the Armed Forces Championships. A few months after that, I was on a date with a girl I had met at the bank. While we were at dinner, a guy came over to our table and started telling his date and mine how I had changed his life by straightening out his diet and helping him with his workouts. My date was flabbergasted and remained so until I showed her photos of days gone by. Moments like that always made me feel like I should have given the sport one more shot. It left me in a funk for a short spell, but it didn't steer me away from my goal in aviation.

As I was pondering my immediate future and enjoying the outdoors waiting for the fish to bite, my cell phone rang. It was one of my former flight instructors calling from the flight school in Warrenton.

"Hey, what are you doing?" he asked.

"Going into a depression," I answered.

"What's the matter?" he asked.

"Nothing. What's up?" I continued.

"Hey remember when we talked about that aerial photography job?" he asked.

He had mentioned a few months earlier that there was a possibility that the U.S. Department of Agriculture was going to contract the flight school to do some aerial photography of various counties in the State of Virginia. It was a golden opportunity for a new commercial pilot to build precious flight time.

"Yeah, what's the word on that?" I queried.

"Can you come out to the airport now?" he asked.

"Yeah sure," I said. I packed up the fishing gear and made my way back to the house. I jumped in the car and sped to the airport.

When I arrived, my former flight instructor was in a heated argument with the guy who ran the flight school. I made my way to a back office and waited for the tension to clear. Ten minutes later the flight instructor burst into the office screaming and cursing. "I'm out of here!" he cried.

"Where are you going?" I asked him.

"I'm going to the airlines, I don't need this!" he answered.

"What about the aerial photo thing?" I asked

He gave me the information on the aerial photography job in rapid fashion and stormed out the door. If I had been late in getting to the airport, I wouldn't have gotten the info, but by the end of the week, I was taking to the skies without having to pay for it.

The Department of Agriculture was playing spy from the sky. Some farmers are on the government subsidy program where they are paid not to farm so as not to have an over abundance of produce; therefore, keeping prices up. Many farmers who are being paid not to farm are harvesting crops off their property and taking them to market to sell. It's double dipping and it's illegal so the Department of Agriculture sends a guy out there to photograph farmland to see who's planting and who's not.

The operation was about as primitive as an octagonal wheel; nevertheless, I was building my flight time. The airplane had a hole cut in the belly and the back seat of the four-seat plane had been removed. We hired a guy to stick a 35mm camera out of the hole and snap photos. It was primitive because there were companies that actually had state of the art equipment to do this, which didn't require an amateur photographer to lie on his stomach with a camera in his hand. The amateur photographer that the flight school hired was so amateur he had never taken photos before.

He was a run of the mill handyman who did various tasks around the airport. He wasn't the brightest bulb in the chandelier; nevertheless, he was given a camera and instructions as to what needed to be done. I explained to him how the operation would go and I followed it up with, "Listen, we're going to be up there for about four hours so if you have to go to the bathroom, now is the time to do it."

We took off into the sky and hadn't been aloft for more than thirty minutes when he asked, "What do I do if I have to pee?"

I closed my eyes, shook my head and asked him, "Were you listening to anything I said back there?"

"I'm sorry. It must be the vibration from the plane," he replied apologetically. "Can't I just pee out of this hole?" he asked referring to the camera hole.

"No!" I replied emphatically. As I began to explain why he couldn't do that, I looked over my seat to see him straddling the hole. Because of the pressure differential between the outside and inside of the plane, the hole actually sucks air into the aircraft. I looked back to see the damage. He was wiping urine from his glasses and the whole back of the plane was soaked. I decided to call it quits and head back to the airport. This guy just didn't understand why the air was being sucked into the plane. He was baffled. As I turned final approach to the runway, he was doing it again with the same result as before. That was the last time the handyman flew with me.

I photographed no less than twenty-five counties across the state. I flew from sun up to sun down every day in the summer as long as the weather cooperated. I logged at least 350 hours that first summer and I didn't have to pay a dime for it. I had left the restaurant business in the dust and opted for a part time mechanic job at the Warrenton Airport. I had a better chance of meeting people that could help further me along in aviation. On many occasions, I bartered my mechanic services for a few free flight hours. I even negotiated a twenty five dollar an hour rental rate on a two seat Cessna so I could continue to build time cheaply when I had to pay for it myself. I regularly flew to Florida on my nights off from American. I would stay on the ground in Florida and sleep in the plane. When I awoke, I would head back to Virginia.

By the end of the first summer of flying aerial photography, I had amassed a total of 700 flight hours. In between the summer months, I continued to barter for flight time as well as pay for it out of my own pocket. No sooner had I made a payment on the credit card I would charge on it again. I was beginning to wonder if I would ever make any substantial money as a commercial pilot.

I was starting to send out résumés for jobs at the commuter airlines and went to a job fair to talk to companies face to face. I handed it to a guy who represented what was probably the worst airline at the commuter level. They offered a starting salary of seventeen thousand dollars a year. He sported a '70s porn star mustache complete with a 'Mike Brady' perm. He smugly told me to call him when I had more flight time. That's another fallacy of the industry. There is a big misconception that the more flight hours you have the better pilot you are. That's not always the case, but that's what I was up against. I couldn't get a job at the worst airline in the country. That crushed me.

My résumé was lacking in total flight time and multi-engine hours. If I could bring those numbers up, more doors would open.

I continued to tell myself that life would get better once I left American. I had arranged my finances so that the only bill I had to pay was the forty thousand dollars of flight training amassed on plastic. I would make the minimum payment until I landed the dream job. That job could be five years down the road if not further. I didn't care. I knew where I wanted to be and I was going to get there no matter what.

I finally got a call from American Eagle Airlines to attend an interview session in Dallas, Texas. It was not my first choice, but I wanted to give it a shot. I studied every aviation book I had and did very well with the technical portion of the interview. I didn't have a single problem until they put me in a Boeing 707 simulator to test my instrument flying abilities. For those of you who don't know, it's a jumbo airliner. I had been flying four and six seat airplanes so I was completely overwhelmed and ended up failing miserably. The whole interview left a bad taste in my mouth. Everything from the arrogant pilots that I met, right down to the other candidates who were just a few months away from carrying that same attitude. I have no idea where that comes from. Today, I am an accomplished Airline Transport Pilot and I don't think I have that "I'm the greatest pilot ever" attitude that these commuter pilots had. I say that laughingly because the commuter airlines were never meant to be a final job stop for a pilot. It is a training ground and one step from the majors. It was all I could do not to laugh when the guy operating the simulator told me that he had been at Eagle for more than five years. If you are at the commuter airlines for more than three years, you either need to re-evaluate your future or just tell everyone that you don't have aspirations to do better. I pondered all of the above while I waited for my flight back home. There is no doubt that I left Dallas with my tail tucked between my legs, but it would take more than that to make me quit!

I received another call for an interview from another low-end commuter airline. Again I failed the simulator test. I was disgusted with myself and was ready to call it quits. I knew I could fly an airplane, but the pressure of flying with someone looking over my shoulder with a job at stake was overwhelming. My friend Chip had passed an interview with Mesaba Airlines and was already flying with them. We talked on the phone quite often. He continued trying to bolster my confidence and told me to keep trying.

I finally nabbed another interview with the commuters. The airline was the now defunct Potomac Airlines based in Roanoke, Virginia. I was hired on the spot without a simulator test. The chief pilot told me that they would get me through the training and that all I needed was a positive attitude. I definitely had that! On the flight home, I went over my finances again. I would be taking a forty thousand dollar a year pay cut. I had it all figured out. Yes it would be a struggle until I got that first pay raise, but it was doable. More importantly, it meant that I would be leaving American airlines.

I immediately typed up my two-week notice and that evening at work I handed it to the supervisor. One of the other mechanics had filled a supervisor position. He was former military so we saw eye to eye on a lot of things. He was affectionately known as Sarge around the maintenance room. He looked at the notice and smiled from ear to ear.

"You finally got it, huh? Congratulations!" he said.

"Hey, Sarge, just in case something goes wrong, maybe I should put in for a leave of absence instead of a resignation. You know, just to cover me," I stated.

He leaned back in his chair and rubbed his hands over his face and then took a deep breath. I knew right then and there he wasn't going to give me that option.

"I'd be more than happy to let you do that, but I'm outnumbered," he said.

He was referring to the other two supervisors who would adamantly refuse my request.

"You've butted heads with those guys too many times and they've already told me there's no way they'll approve it."

I sat there for a minute. "I've got two words for the both of them and I'm sure you know what they are, but it's been great working with you," was my response. He smiled and shook my hand. I cleaned out my locker and for the next two weeks, I made good use of my sick time.

CHAPTER 16

September 11, 2001

I packed everything I owned and jammed it into a small storage facility in Woodbridge, Virginia. I took one last look at it before I closed the door. My heart was pounding. This was the biggest leap I had ever taken. A career change after age thirty was a terrifying thought. What if I flunked out of the school? It was too late to back out now. School started the following day.

It was easier than I thought. I applied myself here just like I had during helicopter mechanic training. I passed with flying colors. The only thing left was the flight training. I was paired up with another new hire and we were scheduled to start our flight training in three days in Charleston, West Virginia. The date was September 10th, 2001.

I called my ex-wife to share the news. We were still close and regularly called one another. She was ecstatic and invited me over to have a visit while I was killing time.

I awoke the next day to the same horrible scene that the rest of the world witnessed. September 11th, 2001: the new Pearl Harbor. It was the day that ruined my life, my career and my future as I had planned it. By noon my phone rang with a call from the chief pilot.

"Listen," he said. "We're not sure what's going to happen right now. Just hang tight, take a few weeks off and we'll call you when we know something ok?"

That's about as positive as anyone could be given the situation. I stayed with my ex-wife until I received the dreaded phone call.

"Is it good news?" I asked.

"No it sure isn't," he said. "The company is going out of business. We're losing a million dollars a day with the planes not flying so the owners are going to pull the plug."

My worst fears were now reality. I started to tally all the money that I had. I withdrew everything from my American Airlines 401k, minus taxes and penalties; I had roughly seven thousand dollars to my name. If I was lucky, it would last me three months.

I sat down and began going over my options when I heard, "They're towing your car!"

I had parked in a tow away zone. I ran outside and caught the guy before he drove off, but it still cost me sixty five dollars to get my car back. My ex-wife tried to console me. "Don't worry, everything is going to work out," she told me.

I exploded into a rage. "It's not going to work out! I don't have any money and I certainly didn't have any money for that!" I was reduced to tears. I sat down and cried as my world crumbled.

I reflected back on the day when I was sharing breakfast with Bench Man. This was the same moment that he had experienced in his life. This is where he threw in the towel. I understood why. I felt alone against the world. It took every ounce of inner strength I could muster to prevent the events in my life from breaking me down completely.

I packed up my belongings and told my ex-wife thanks for everything. If there was one thing in this world that I could count on it was her friendship. I loaded my car and hugged her goodbye. She had never seen me beaten down to this level before and I could see the sadness and doubt in her eyes. We both knew that I had a long road ahead.

I once again found myself in the unemployment line. The government was a bit more sympathetic to my situation this time. The representative told me that I was entitled to three hundred and sixty eight dollars a week as a larger amount had been authorized due to the circumstances. On top of that, I was again working as a mechanic under the table. I even finished the tail end of the Department of Agriculture contract, which allowed me to keep flying.

At this point, I was living in my car. Everything I owned was still in storage. I had a handful of clothes and some toiletries. My car was a two-door hatchback and with my belongings piled up in the back seat, I had to sleep with the seat almost upright. I spent the night parked at the local rest stop. In the morning, I cleaned up by washing at the sink in the rest stop bathroom. I looked around at the other vehicles that were parked near me. They had clothes stacked upon clothes and suitcases and stuff strewn throughout. I wondered if they were in the same situation as me. You've heard the phrase "hitting rock bottom?" I had just gone two feet deeper than that. I was scared to death of what my future might hold. I let people believe that I had a place to stay and that things were going just fine. I wasn't looking for sympathy or handouts so I kept my situation to myself.

When I left American, our union was in the process of negotiating a new contract. It had been ongoing for over a year. I got a call from one of the guys saying that the contract had been settled and that everyone was getting a retroactive paycheck. That meant that I would get a back check for the amount of the difference between what I was making when I left and the new raise for a period of seven months. It amounted to almost seven thousand dollars. I took the money and purchased a used motor home.

I continued to turn wrenches for cash and I collected the unemployment for as long as I could. During the holidays of that year, I helped a local crop duster by flying him to and from different locations across the state. I also worked as his one-man ground crew. I loaded the fertilizer truck then positioned it to load the airplane when it landed. I was basically his pit crew keeping him fueled and loaded with fertilizer from sun up to sun down. I also relocated the equipment from airport to airport sometimes driving well into the night so we could get an early start the following day. I had fun doing it, but it was back breaking work. I did what I had to do as flying jobs were not to be had. The industry had thousands on furlough and it was going to be a long time before hiring would commence again.

My big break came when we were working out of a small airport just east of Richmond, Virginia. In between keeping my crop dusting friend in the sky and keeping the fertilizer truck at the ready, I was trying to find an oil leak on the airplane that we used to travel to and from the job sites. The airplane hadn't been sitting for more than an hour and it already had a puddle of oil under it. I turned my hat around and went to work. About that time, I heard a voice behind me.

"Hey are you a mechanic? I could sure use one," the voice said.

I didn't look up from what I was doing. "I'm not really interested in being a mechanic. I'm looking to fly," I said.

"Well, I actually need mechanics and pilots," he added. "So you're a pilot too?"

I looked up and told him yes. He gave me a number to the Director of Operations for his charter company, which was based just south of Richmond in Petersburg, Virginia. I made the call, which landed me an interview, which in turn landed me the job. I loaded up the gypsy motor home and departed the airport lot in Warrenton only to relocate to another airport lot in Petersburg. I was going to get back into the sky on a full time basis and get paid to do it. The money would amount to thirty thousand dollars a year, but I would also have to pull duty as a mechanic. It was a small price to pay to fly again.

The Director of Operations was a down home country boy named Pete. He was a former corporate pilot who was no longer looking to fly. He treasured his time at home with his family and his hobby of training horses. Pete had been a renowned horse trainer before his days of flying and he was slowly returning to his old ways. He did his nine to five at the office and left the flying to the younger guys who were looking to build their résumés. We became close friends and I have him to thank for more than one big break.

The owner however, was something else. He was a used car salesman disgracing the world of aviation with his shyster techniques. He was exactly what I loathed about the pilot corps. His parents had nursed him well past the age of eighteen. They sent him to rich kid college and even after graduating, rumor had it that they continued to give him an allowance. He was the best pilot he knew and he would tell you about it every chance he could. When he introduced himself and this is the absolute truth, he would say, "Hi I'm so and so, I'm an F-16 fighter pilot." Once, in a moment of perceived profundity, he told me, "You know, you and I aren't that far apart. I was just given better opportunities in life." He had no clue what life was like without the protection and comfort of his parents' wings.

The airplanes at this company were in haphazard condition. The owner instilled the same techniques buying airplanes that he did buying cars. If it had a pretty paint job, he would buy it. We had planes that had cracks in the wings and cracks on the main spar, which is the one-piece beam that holds the wings to the aircraft. He also didn't put any emphasis on proper and responsible maintenance. On one occasion, I had to make an emergency landing because one of my engines was sputtering. I was flying a passenger to Grand Rapids, Michigan in the middle of the night and just as we passed over the mountains the engine caused a vibration that shook the whole plane. The other pilot and I decided to land in Parkersburg, West Virginia. Since both of us were mechanics, we investigated the problem in depth and found that someone in the maintenance shop had left rags in the fuel tanks. The fuel decomposed the threads, which then clogged every part of the fuel system.

Most of the flying was done in the middle of the night and in the worst of weather. It was definitely a job where I learned some valuable lessons; the first being, never, ever go flying with an aircraft owner-pilot. The only reason this guy asked you to go in the first place is because he has no clue what he's doing. You're not a pilot at this point you're a babysitter. I made that mistake with the owner of a twin engine Cessna. This guy was at least 70 years old and I was told that he was a competent pilot and just wanted someone to sit in the right seat to make sure he didn't do something "stupid."

We flew to Poughkeepsie, New York and back to Petersburg. The weather in Petersburg had gone sour by the time we arrived late at night. As I listened on the radio for the latest weather report, I cringed when I heard the voice say that the weather was about one hundred feet above the minimums for the approach. Simply put, this meant that when we broke out of the bottom of the clouds we would be about six hundred feet above the ground. The winds were at least thirty knots and it was raining. The worst of all of this was that the approach was known as a circling approach, which meant that when you broke out of the clouds, you had to circle to the other end of the runway to land. Many airplanes had crashed performing this very type of maneuver in these exact conditions.

As we began the approach, he turned us to the right, which was correct; however, he didn't correct for the wind so instead of turning approximately thirty degrees to the right of the desired course we went about sixty degrees. We flew this heading for the prescribed one minute and then turned back towards the runway. On a perfect day with no wind we would have been lined up with the runway so that when we broke out of the clouds a beautiful piece of pavement would have welcomed us home. Again, he didn't correct for the wind, which put us lined up in the direction of the runway, but at least a half-mile to the left of it. I caught the mistake after he had made the turn.

"Turn forty degrees to the right!" I hollered into my microphone. "We didn't correct for the wind!" I continued. "Fly to the marker!" The marker is a radio beacon aligned with and preceding the runway. This would at least put us at a known point because as it was, we were still in the clouds and well to the left of course. I didn't know the exact location of our aircraft in reference to the runway. He turned the airplane for the marker and tracked it. When the needle on our cockpit gage flipped, I knew we were on top of the radio beacon. Understand that while all this confusion was going on, the wind was tossing the aircraft all over the place and the rain was pounding us so hard it sounded like rocks hitting the plane. This only exacerbated the feeling of panic. He turned toward the prescribed heading and began the final descent to the runway again not correcting for the wind. I knew that on one side of the runway there were buildings and on the other there were trees. We were on course to descend into the trees! I took control of the airplane and turned us thirty degrees to the right. We broke out of the clouds roughly six hundred feet above the ground as we had expected, but the only thing I saw were the lights of the buildings to the right.

"Where's the runway?" I asked in sheer panic.

"It's over to the left," he answered.

"Don't lose sight of it!" I turned the plane further to the right as I was too close to make a safe turn to land.

"I think I just lost sight of it," he said in a voice that was too calm for the situation at hand. I yanked the airplane into a sixty degree bank back toward the runway. I saw the lights that lined the edge, but I was too high to land. I pulled the power to idle, but the wind kept me afloat halfway down the runway. I finally slammed the plane on the deck and jumped on the brakes. We came to rest a mere fifty feet from the end of the strip. A lesson learned.

I sold the RV and paid down a little bit of my immense debt. No sooner had I paid some of it down, I charged it right back up when I decided to pursue my college degree through an online course. I just didn't have the funds to pay for it outright. I was still living paycheck to paycheck.

My debt only became worse when I received a letter from the Internal Revenue Service stating that there was some kind of error on my taxes. I was hit hard with taxes from 2001. I had withdrawn my retirement funds, which acquired heavy penalties, but now there was something amiss, which was going to cause even bigger problems. All those hours of whoring myself out as a mechanic to the maintenance shop in Warrenton had been worked with the understanding that it was going to be under the table. I felt completely betrayed when the IRS said that the employer had reported all of those wages. I couldn't believe that the guy who ran the shop did that to me. He never even sent me a 1099 form. Not only would I get hammered from the IRS, but I had to contend with the folks from unemployment as well. I received that phone call a few weeks later. All said and done, the grand total from fines, fees and back taxes was five thousand dollars. I added it to the forty thousand that I already owed.

We flew a lot of hours the first six months that I was there, but the flying soon tapered off mainly due to the fact that the planes were pieces of junk. It became increasingly difficult to keep them safe for flight. I was spending most of my time working in the maintenance shop. Over the course of the year, I had accumulated another six hundred hours of flight time. I was ready to advance to the next step in my career, but aviation hadn't begun to recover. Pilots were still being furloughed.

I made the decision to forego any aspirations of becoming an airline pilot. My age was a limiting factor. I would need to get hired by the time I was forty. That would give me twenty years of a good salary before mandatory retirement at age sixty. I was already in my mid thirties. If I went to work for the regional airlines, I would be a co-pilot for at least five years before I would make captain. In order to be a competitive candidate for getting hired by the major airlines, you need captain flight time under your belt. By the time I would have achieved that, I would be 43 or 44 years old. There was also the money issue. I couldn't survive on a regional airline pilot's starting salary of twenty thousand dollars a year. I took another approach to the situation.

CHAPTER 17

Into Parts Unknown

I stumbled across an ad from a company looking for pilot-mechanics. I knew the company flew jet prop airplanes so I sent them my résumé. I was very persistent and actually sent them one a month until they finally called. I knew I was qualified to do the job. The interview was nothing too difficult and I even passed the simulator test. That was a big step for me. I asked them after I interviewed what their criteria were for hiring and the lead interviewer smiled and said, "Mr. Fett, in your case, it was persistence." He had all four of the résumés I sent sitting in front of him. If there's a door you think should be behind you instead of in your face, knock a few times, if they don't answer, kick it down. I signed on accepting rock bottom wages, the most dangerous flying in the civilian world with the possibility of being gone for months at a time. I used vacation time from the job in Petersburg to attend the initial training. Afterwards, I jumped ship and took up residence in a tiny one-bedroom apartment in Harrisonburg, Virginia.

The apartment complex was run down. The neighborhood was in the low rent district and was comprised of mostly college students attending James Madison University. The town was also home to a very large Hispanic population that kept the local turkey factory supplied with cheap labor. Many of them lived in the same complex. I didn't care who my neighbors were since I was going to be on the road most of the time.

Harrisonburg had little to offer in the form of entertainment. Again, it was a college town so it was populated with college bars, which offered nothing but ditzy babes, a cloud of smoke, and bad karaoke. The only place I liked to hang out was a restaurant/bar called Calhoun's featuring great food, hot waitresses, and live music.

The airplanes were old military U-21's. A small twin-engine, unpressurized vessel that could seat eight people comfortably if they were passenger transports; these planes were anything but that. Most of the planes were empty shells that were used for everything from photography equipment to chemical holding tanks used for spraying. We did aerial land surveying, night-vision goggle insect spraying, aerial photography with state of the art equipment, and we provided airplanes for the Bureau of Land Management to use during forest fire season.

I spent my first three weeks on the job flying in Southern California. I was flying an old Beechcraft that had been converted from radial engines to turbine engines and I was taking part in what was known as sterile insect technique. In layman's terms, I was dropping sterile flies over the land. The theory here was that by introducing sterile fruit flies to the environment, they would not be able to reproduce yet the proper balance of the eco system wouldn't be knocked out of whack as it surely would have had we used insecticides to eliminate the flies. Evidently it worked, but frankly, I could care less. I was finally flying a plane with jet prop engines.

I had a blast flying low level over the Los Angeles basin. One of the guys that I flew with would always turn the aircraft on its side when we flew over the playboy mansion.

"Any girls down there?" he would ask.

The plane was one wing to the ground with the other straight up to the sky and my face was plastered against the window in the hopes of catching a glimpse, but flying by at 200 mph doesn't really give you time to focus.

When I wasn't flying, I was in the maintenance shop getting dirty with the other mechanics. These guys were great mechanics and down to earth honest guys. If something wasn't right, they spoke up or they made it right. They cared and I considered it a privilege to be working with them. No union here. As for the management, it wasn't up to my standards. The shop foreman was a blithering idiot. The rumor was that as a mechanic he broke more than he fixed so they made him the foreman in an attempt to stop the destruction. It put to practice the adage of those who can, do. Those who can't, supervise.

The owner of the company had a serious problem with micro managing and an inability to delegate. He had to make decisions regarding everything. Most CEO's sit in their offices and make decisions that concern money, new customers, new contracts, etc. This guy was down on the maintenance floor telling guys which parts to change and how to change them, which completely defeated the purpose of having floor managers.

The flying at this company was by far the most exhilarating and the most dangerous I have ever experienced. We performed low level insect spraying at night with the aid of night vision goggles. The majority of my flying here was done only a hundred feet above the ground!

After the job in Southern California, I was sent to finish a project in Arizona. We were doing aerial surveying for a client that was trying to assess land damage after a forest fire. I was working out of Show Low, a small town that made Camanche look like a jumping metropolis! When you're feeling depressed and you need a lift, visit Show Low. You'll realize how good you have it.

Upon returning to Virginia, I became part of a project that involved an experimental airplane and a 6-week journey to the great white arctic regions of northern Canada. The airplane was a new venture for the company. They had modified one of the planes into a flying magnetometer. The conceptual design was to attach magnetic sensors extending from the tail and both wings. When it was completed, the wings had three foot extensions with what looked like footballs sticking out from the ends and the tail had a tubular boom that extended approximately seven feet from the end of the plane. I affectionately referred to the plane as The Diamond Hunter since that was the purpose of its design.

The meat of the process was that a rock formation called Kimberlyte was generally found around diamond deposits. Kimberlyte has a very high magnetic property hence the magnetic sensors on the plane. I fly the aircraft at very low altitudes so that the sensors can pick up magnetic readings from the earth. The sensors feed into the computers installed in the back of the plane for the engineers to evaluate. If something looks positive, they set up mining teams for core samples and further research.

The day that my journey started from Virginia was like any in aviation. You try to plan everything precisely, but invariably everything goes wrong. The original plan was for me to fly the commercial airlines to the arctic and meet the plane there, but the plan fell through. Plan B was put together at the last minute and it called for me to fly the plane to the arctic. The whole thing became a rush-rush hurry up deal.

When I arrived at the airport to start my preflight preparations, the airplane had already been loaded, or rather overloaded. I would estimate that the craft was five hundred pounds overweight. It wasn't a big deal except that the runway was short. The situation was made worse with the fact that it was a hot August day, which meant that the engines wouldn't perform at peak performance. I climbed up into the plane and taxied down to the runway end. I could feel how heavy the craft was which gave me doubts whether or not I would be able to get airborne before the end of the runway. I sat at the end and ran the engines to full power. I held the brakes until the gages said she was ready. When I released them, the plane didn't jump forward like she would have if she'd been lighter. I didn't even look at the instrument panel. The end of the runway was coming up fast. I pulled back on the yoke and the nose slowly and lethargically lumbered into the sky. Not a moment too soon either as, at that point, I was at the end of the runway.

My first stop was London, Ontario. I arrived in the midst of thunderstorms and had to fly the approach. I cleared customs there and within thirty minutes, I was breaking away from the ground again and headed to Stratford, Ontario. The weather here was worse than London and I had to fly yet another approach, this time to the minimum altitude before I found the runway. This is where I spent the night. The client had at least two days worth of work to perform on the plane installing more equipment. In the mean time, I called my contact in Toronto who was tasked with educating me on the finer points of flying in the arctic. She had prior experience.

She picked me up late at night and drove me to Toronto, which was about an hour and forty minutes. When she showed up, she handed me a bag full of maps. Throughout the course of the trip she began rambling about the rules of arctic flying. Have you ever seen a boxer listening to his trainer at the beginning of round eleven? That was me, dazed and confused from a long day of traveling; nothing she said registered in my head. I wasn't any better off when I departed Stratford than before I had arrived.

After two days of down time, the client and I lumbered into the sky bound for Geraldton, Ontario, which was located northeast of Thunderbay. If my plane had been five hundred pounds overweight leaving Virginia, it was now one thousand pounds overweight leaving Stratford. The client had added food that we couldn't get up north plus his personal affects as well as the computer equipment that was now installed in the back.

Geraldton was as far as the trip was going to go that day due to bad weather. We both agreed that it was a good place to stay. The town had a hotel and food, which was all we needed. I put the airplane to bed for the night.

The following day we were off the ground bright and early. The foul weather had passed and the forecast for the rest of the journey was clear blue skies. I wanted to make our destination by nightfall. Our next stop was Churchill, Manitoba.

It was seasonably warm; sixty degrees on the Fahrenheit scale. The terrain beneath us up to this point was densely populated with forests, but was slowly giving way to flatter, more barren land. Lakes were appearing like magic. Everywhere I looked there was a lake. I spotted Churchill's runway from miles away. When we landed, I had to change the settings in my GPS instrumentation since we were now flying above the 60-degree parallel. It was previously set for magnetic compass settings, but north of the 60-degree line meant that magnetic compasses couldn't be used with reliability due to the earth's strong magnetic field. The wet compass in the window was roughly 40-degrees off.

Next stop was Rankin Inlet. The flight from Churchill to the inlet was awe-inspiring! I flew along the northwest edge of the great Hudson Bay. Land littered with hundreds of lakes lay to my left and the beautiful water of the bay on my right. We were on schedule and would make our destination of Iglulik, Nunavut as planned.

In Rankin, we fueled the plane and took a quick break. We also took on another passenger. He was a company mechanic that had volunteered for the arctic assignment. As I left the passenger terminal building, I noticed Inuit writings on the wall. I have no idea what it said, but it reminded me of ancient hieroglyphics. We weren't in Kansas anymore.

I climbed up into the plane and looked behind me. I could barely see my two passengers buried under all of our gear. I shook my head as we taxied out for the final leg. At this point, I was going to be a test pilot. There wasn't anything in the aircraft manuals that told me how to fly this airplane in its current loaded condition. Much to my surprise and profound happiness, she rolled down the runway and shot into the sky.

It was somewhere between Rankin Inlet and Iglulik that the world to my left was turning white. The lakes were ice-covered in some parts and the terrain had changed to a rugged, jagged rock devoid of any plant life. I might as well have been on the moon or Mars for all the miles and miles of nothingness. I was completely overcome with a feeling of privilege that I was one of the few in this world who got to see such a sight.

I didn't pick up the runway in Iglulik until we were ten miles out. In my defense, it was a runway only in the sense that it was used as a place to land a plane. In the state of Iowa we would have called it a country gravel road and from the sky it looked like a sidewalk. As I rounded the tip of the island, I saw people on the beach nestled around little shanties.

"That is the nude beach down there!" hollered the client. He was a thin Pakistani man sporting a full beard. He laughed at his own joke. "You won't like the women when you first see them, but in three weeks, you'll change your mind." We all laughed at that. Those were words to live by in the north. I turned onto the final approach for the gravel runway. The sun was hanging in the lower quarter of the sky and our fourteen hour journey had come to a close.

Iglulik, sometimes spelled Igloolik, means "there is an igloo here," but there were none to be seen on this day as the temperature outside was at least sixty degrees. It was a pleasant surprise as all of my preconceptions of the arctic led me to believe that this place was always dastardly cold.

There was a small school and a hotel that resembled a doublewide trailer. The most up to date building was the government complex. The settlement also had a police station that housed the Royal Canadian Mounted Police and about half way down the main dirt thoroughfare were two co-ops where we bought our supplies. On top of the rocky cliff to the north of town was a graveyard; one in which the deceased were covered with rocks above ground since the ground was frozen.

One surprising fact about the far north is that there is no shortage of mosquitoes. The many lakes up there provide a perfect breeding ground. They came out in swarms. I immediately put on my sweatshirt and pulled the hood over my head. The mechanic pulled out a jacket that had been designed for just such a problem. It resembled a beekeeper's suit with mesh around the face yet it was lightweight and comfortable. "I was ready for this!" he exclaimed.

I was swatting in all directions. Thankfully there were days when the wind was strong enough to keep the mosquitoes at bay, but there were also times when I ran from the airport to the house to try to keep them off.

The accommodations were better than expected. The client had rented a three-bedroom house that was in the middle of the settlement and about a fifteen-minute walk from the airport. We shared the house with a group of Canadian pilots as well. When it came to keeping our living quarters clean, we were on the lower side of the grading curve. We were definitely hampered by the fact that we were unable to enjoy what I would call basic living necessities. Water, for instance, was limited. In the arctic, it's impossible to have water lines running through the ground. There were no sewer systems either. The houses were built on stilts. This was to combat the problem of ice breaking into large plates when the spring temperatures started thawing the winter deposits. The plates had been known to slide downhill and crash into houses or worse yet carry it the same as a mudslide would. Putting the houses on stilts allowed the ice plates to slide under without causing damage. The floors were wood and it was a never-ending task to keep them cleaned since our boots were always filthy from walking on the settlement's dirt roads. You didn't dare walk around the house with bare feet!

To solve the problem of not having water on demand, every house had a storage tank inside. Ours was a 250-gallon tank mounted to the wall of the utility room. We had six guys doing dishes, laundry and taking showers. How long do you think 250 gallons lasted us? When we needed the tank replenished, we turned on a light located on the outside of the house to let the water delivery guy know we needed more water. We did the same to have the septic tank serviced.

I will be the first to tell you that I am a bit obsessive-compulsive when it comes to cleanliness so when I first stepped into the house, I almost had a nervous breakdown. I unloaded my gear and started settling into a bedroom, which I shared with the mechanic. We both were dying for a hot shower and I graciously let him go first while I went out to the living room to get acquainted with our Canadian brethren.

When the bathroom was made available, I grabbed a towel and breathed a sigh of relief. My roommate stopped me with these words.

"Dude, that place is filthy, beware of the shower curtain!"

I shook my head. "You've got to be kidding me."

"Best of luck," he replied.

I cautiously opened the door and slowly crept in. I was mortified. The walls were yellow with streaks of nicotine from cigarette smoke. The sink had soap scum that almost disguised the original color of the basin. The mirror was so dirty I couldn't see my reflection and there aren't words in the English language to describe the condition of the toilet. It was a tiny motor home styled toilet that wasn't even permanently fixed to the floor. When you sat on this thing, you had to sit still otherwise you ran the risk of tipping over. A house full of guys and not one of them could pee in a pool if they were standing on the edge of one. The seat and the bowl and the floor were riddled with urine. As I pulled the shower curtain back, the overhead light revealed a bathtub coated with green algae slime. There must have been fifteen bottles of various shampoos and conditioners nestled in the corners of the tub and the wall behind them was black from mold. The shower curtain had the same algae slime covering the inside of it. I stepped back out of the bathroom and grabbed five more towels. I placed two around the floor of the toilet and one in front of the tub. I placed one on the sink so I could put my toiletries on top of it and the other I kept in my hand suspended above my head while I showered. It was all I could do to keep the shower curtain from clinging to my legs as I moved around. I could feel the slime every time it touched me. I finally had to throw the curtain on the outside of the tub, but as I finished and was about to step out, I could see that the water that went outside of the tub had washed around the toilet therefore freeing the yellowness around the base. If I was going to step out into that, I might as well have stuck my feet into the toilet directly. I threw down the towel that I had in my hand and leaped across the yellow pond. I got dressed with water dripping off of me, brushed my teeth and crawled into bed.

"Well?" he asked as I rolled over burying myself under the covers.

"Unbelievable," was all I could say. We both laughed at the situation we were in.

CHAPTER 18

Arctic Life

The way of life in the arctic would take some getting used to, but I was handling it well, except for the fact that it was light twenty four hours a day. We had to cover the windows so that we could sleep because 2:00 a.m. looked like 4:00 p.m. The Inuit (Eskimo) children never went indoors. They played in the schoolyard across the street all through what I considered to be nighttime. After the first week, I no longer kept track of time. I went to sleep when I was tired since it wasn't going to get dark to remind me that it was time for bed. Our client never quite figured it out either. The first day we were there, he came over to the house at 1:00 a.m. requesting that we go flying. I looked at my roommate.

"Is he kidding?" I asked.

"I think he's serious," he answered. We looked at each other and with heavy sighs headed off to work. My roommate always went to the airport with me. He made sure the plane was mechanically sound and helped with refueling as this had become a chore. Gone were the days of having a guy in a truck drive up to the plane and start pumping gas. We were pumping our fuel out of fifty gallon drums with a small electric pump. The process took about forty five minutes and that included removing the drums from the pallets and returning them empty. We also had to put covers on the engines and the tail and wing surfaces to protect them from the high winds and snow. Though the temperatures were spring-like when we arrived, they would change by the end of the week.

Flying that experimental plane in a part of the world that I had only seen pictures of was truly marvelous. It was also the most dangerous flying that I have ever done. My options were limited if something went wrong. I had one alternate airport to the south if the weather didn't allow me to land in Iglulik and the weather was always an issue that I had to deal with. I didn't have access to up-to-the-minute radar pictures and the high tech equipment that most pilots are afforded. I had telephone access to a guy who was interpreting weather prognostic charts that were twelve hours old and he was located in a city hours away from me.

The flying was to be at one hundred feet and in the neighborhood of one hundred and fifty knots. I had two altimeters in the plane and both were located on the panel directly in front of me. The most important one was my radio altimeter, which told my altitude in reference to my height above ground. It was equipped with an audible alarm in the event that I strayed below my target altitude. We had modified the instrument panel so that this altimeter was directly in front of my face.

The terrain on Baffin Island was absolutely rugged with jagged rocks and mountains. I would have to fly over these at one hundred feet as well as deal with the fifty to sixty mph winds that ripped between the high peaks. The first flight was a practice run to bolster my self-confidence. We chose a small parcel of land on the east side of Baffin Island just to the north of Iglulik. I was able to locate the area known as the survey block on both my paper maps and the GPS. I was never afraid of getting lost, just afraid of smashing the plane into a big rock.

Our client had the survey block divided into lines that were various miles in length and equidistant laterally. His computer was tied into a light bar that sat on the top portion of my instrument panel. The light bar had a series of red digital lights with a line drawn down the center separating left from right. If a red light appeared on the right side, it meant that you were a little off the course line; steer right. If a lot of lights appeared, it meant you were way off. It was the same system that many crop dusters use. All I had to do was follow the lights to stay on the course line. The bar also had a kilometer read out, which cued me in as to when the line was ending. I chased the lights from side to side initially, but eventually settled in to where there wasn't a light on the bar.

The computer system's magnetic sensors were very sensitive to electrical interference. I had to shut off one engine generator, the aircraft's lights, and all but one radio. This also prevented me from making any throttle changes. Moving the throttles caused an electrical current that the sensors were able to record; therefore, changing my engine power setting was a no-no unless it was an emergency. If I moved the throttles, we would have to fly that particular line over. If it was one hundred kilometers long, we just wasted a lot of time and money so it was important to adhere to protocol.

The first time that I flew with the intent of recording the data was a gut wrenching experience. The terrain was laid out like a skateboard half pipe; high on both ends with the middle being a valley. The line distance was about sixty kilometers. I set power so that I would be a little fast diving into the valley, but hopefully enough to keep me safely above stall speed at the end where I would be nose up and climbing. The wind was ripping across the jagged rocks and it was taking everything I had to control the plane. When I dove downward into the valley, I was dead on the line and right at altitude. I was hugging the surface of the earth with a one hundred-foot buffer. The wind forced me to steer the airplane approximately thirty five degrees to one side, which actually had me flying sideways. As the terrain progressed upwards near the end of the line, I brought the nose up to preserve my altitude. Bringing the nose up meant that I would have to increase power to maintain my speed. I knew that that would force us to have to fly the line again since it would require a throttle change. I watched my airspeed slowly fall off. I looked at the light bar to see that I had four kilometers to go till the end of the line. The plane was pointed twelve degrees nose up and the airspeed was teetering on stall speed. By the time I finished the line, I wouldn't have enough speed to keep the plane flying. Swallow my pride and move the throttles, or fall out of the sky and no one would know the difference! Decisions, decisions. I was going to have to make one quickly. I swallowed my pride and reached for the throttles, but just as I grabbed them, the airplane nose went down and the audible alarm from my radio altimeter sounded. I glanced at it and realized that I had flown directly into a downdraft. The altimeter read sixty feet and the gages indicated that she was still going down towards the rocks! I pulled the nose up and a wicked burst of air shot me out over the edge of the cliff, which by coincidence was also the end of the course line. I cleared the rocks by about fifty feet. I climbed up to a thousand feet above the terrain and slammed the plane into a forty five degree bank to the right. I counted twenty-five seconds, then banked it hard over to sixty degrees to the left. I was looking down at a river that nestled itself between the cliffs approximately four thousand feet below. The lights on the bar came into center and I leveled the wings. I was still holding a thirty five degree turn into the wind to stay on the course line as Mother Nature rocked the craft mercilessly. I was just inside one kilometer to the start of the new line and I was descending to my target altitude. I've heard the fighter pilot stories of flying low and fast, but until you've flown sideways directly at a mountain's edge in moderate turbulence trying to cross over that edge at one hundred feet, you haven't flown. By the time we had completed the surveying on Baffin Island, my nerves were shot. I had plenty of confidence, but this style of flying was meant for the "young and dumbs," not a guy in his thirties.

The greatest obstacle in arctic flying is the weather. The local Canadian pilots would tell you, "if it's forecasting fog, stay close to home because it moves fast and stays a while." Without an instrument approach to Iglulik's airport, fog would keep us grounded for days. If you were out flying when the fog arrived, you wouldn't be able to get back in so things like being low on fuel and the lack of an alternate airport would cause a crisis. This was in the back of my mind when we launched out across the Foxe Basin to survey a small island.

The basin was the immense body of water that lay to the south of Iglulik. The sky was overcast at about two thousand feet with scattered clouds below. I slipped across the water at a thousand feet. There were snow cells scattered all around us and I could see to the northeast that snow was already blanketing the coastline. The survey block lay to the southeast about twenty minutes from base. I was well aware that the forecast was for the weather to go sour in the next few hours so I had made a prior arrangement with a local helicopter pilot that if the weather in Iglulik goes belly up, call me on the radio.

I weaved my way between the snow showers and ducked under a wall of low clouds before entering the block. I was relieved to see that the land was completely flat and the wind was minimal. In my mind, this was easy money. I was keeping a close eye on the island of Iglulik. Various snow showers had popped up in all quadrants of my airspace. The snow was closing in on the block and was literally chasing me as I progressed across the island. As I made my turns on the north end, my wing dipped into the clouds and snow pelted the window. I looked down at the ground through my side window to give me some sort of reference as to my position relative to the earth. As I rolled out to start the next course line the visibility was endless! That's how it went until I heard the crackle of static on the radio. It was the helicopter pilot warning me that the weather in Iglulik had deteriorated. The snow cells over the water had obscured my view of the settlement and the sheer excitement of flying had steered my thoughts. The fog was moving in from the north and I heard "one and a half miles visibility" over the frequency. I hollered to my Pakistani friend in back that we needed to return to base immediately.

I tried to track back the same way we came, but the snow showers had intensified and forced me further north. The only way to stay out of the fog was to stay below it. Being twenty minutes from Iglulik with impending fog was unnerving, but complicating matters was the fact that I was twenty minutes out, over water, and flying at four hundred feet. I contacted the airport observer.

"What's the visibility?" I asked.

"It's down to a mile," he replied.

There are three things in aviation that are useless: altitude above you, runway behind you, and the fuel you didn't get. On this day, I was sure I had found a fourth. I had plenty of fuel and no place to land. I was ten minutes out and my flight visibility was two miles and diminishing. I slowed the machine down so I could see what was ahead. I was coming in from the northeast, which was a little bit foreign to me since most of our previous work had been conducted to the south. I strained to see anything below me, but I was still over the water. I kept looking for the settlement. Most of the buildings were bright blues and oranges. This helped the Inuit hunters find home on days like today and I was hoping it would do the same for me. Fortunately, I had state of the art instrumentation and I was fully prepared to fly a homemade approach if it came to that. The fog had devoured the world to my right. "Where is the coastline?" I asked myself. Just then I had a glimpse of a blue building and Iglulik was coming into view. I was still holding four hundred feet of altitude and I didn't want to descend further for fear of hitting a radio antenna. There were a few in the vicinity of the airport. Since I was approaching from the north, the runway would be off to my left. I had loaded my homemade approach into the GPS and began to fly it. I turned a two-mile final and began a slow descent. I caught glimpses of the ground as the earth closed the space between us, but I didn't gain sight of the runway until I was three-quarter mile from touchdown. I took a deep breath and recollected another favorite aviation saying: "I'd rather be down here wishing I was up there, than be up there wishing I was down here." As we refueled the aircraft, the What Ifs danced about in my head. I was the only one who knew how close we had come to not being able to find the airport.

When we arrived back at the house, my thoughts turned to the Canadian crew. Had they made it back? I looked out the front window and watched the fog engulf house after house in the settlement. The scene was right out of a Stephen King movie. If they hadn't made it back by now, there was no way they were going to get in. Just then though, the front door opened.

"That fog is moving fast, eh?" the pilot stated in that familiar Canuck statement-question. "We made it in right after you."

I was relieved to know that everybody had made it on the ground safely. The fog covered Iglulik for three days. We passed the time playing video games and watching television.

I normally flew two flights a day each of them roughly four hours in length, while the Canadian team flew twelve hours or more. They had two pilots. When the day was over, we had sit-down meals. We shared stories of things we had done and places that we had been. I really enjoyed it and became very fond of the Canadians. All of our meals were all you can eat. Whatever we wanted and as long as it was on the shelves of the co-op, it was fair game. We had a running tab down there and we didn't have to pay for it! The client had a local woman stop by and fix us dinner on occasion, but more often than not we were able to fend for ourselves.

The Inuit people were very friendly to me even though most didn't speak English. They lived in houses that were equivalent to any you would see in a low-income neighborhood in any U.S. city. Most owned four wheelers and snowmobiles. Some owned boats and on the other side of the island some of the hunters had dog sleds.

It wasn't long before the twenty-four hours of light subsided to the point where we were experiencing about six hours of darkness. This is when Iglulik came to life! I took a stroll to see what I could see after hours and came to the realization that the Arctic let its hair down in the dark. There were people falling down drunk in the streets and partying in the doorways and porches of the houses. It was against the law to have alcohol in the settlement, but that didn't stop the Inuit. You could always find booze; you just had to ask the right person. We joked about the number of people that showed up to greet the commercial flights when they arrived. The flight carried only a handful of passengers, but forty people showed up to greet them. We were told that they were picking up "care packages" sent from southern Canada that contained liquor and even marijuana. I didn't believe it until a local craftsman stopped by the house to ask if anyone wanted a souvenir carving made from a walrus tusk.

He reminded me of Tom Sawyer's Injun Joe only much shorter. He had the same leather hat and wild jet-black hair. His clothes resembled more of a Native American than any preconceived Eskimo picture in my mind. He spoke English fairly well, but he spoke slowly and with pause as if he were thinking and focusing on every word. His delivery was in a guttural tone.

The craftsman stopped by our house and gave his best sales pitch. He had samples of his work and I must say he was a very talented artist. He convinced a few of the guys to have him create animal carvings for them with one catch and that was an up-front partial payment. I backed away from that. They gave the man the required deposit stating, "Dude, we're on an island in the Arctic, where's he going to run off to?" It was a valid point, but it was becoming suspect at the end of the week when the artist didn't deliver the goods as promised.

Two of the prospective buyers decided to walk down to his house and see what was holding things up. They knocked on the door, but no answer. They knocked again only louder. Still no answer, but they heard the sound of footsteps running through the house. Up the stairs, then back down, but still no answer. They finally saw the artist peeking through the curtains. He recognized them and opened the door. He was standing in the doorway in his underwear telling the guys that he had been smoking marijuana and thought that it was the Royal Canadian Mounted Police knocking on his door. He offered them some pot, but the guys kindly refused and departed with reassurances that their carvings would be ready at the end of the week. When Friday arrived, the artist delivered with top quality items. We later found out that this guy only came around when he needed money to buy his dope!

My trip to Iglulik lasted about six weeks before I was relieved of duty. I flew back to Virginia on a commercial flight in an old beat up turbo prop plane. It was half full of cargo and half full of people. The props made an awful sound for the duration of the two-hour flight to Iqaluit. This is where I connected to another flight to take me to Toronto and then to Washington D.C. where I drove the final two hours home.

Though the flight was loud and the aircraft old and rickety, I looked out of the window down to where the world was turning white and reflected back on everything that I had just experienced. I grinned from ear to ear with the thought that there were very few people in this world that could say they had done this.

CHAPTER 19

Rattled Nerves

I was slowly putting my life back together. My finances were straightening out and I had reduced my debt from forty thousand dollars to thirty thousand. I made frequent phone calls to family to tell them that I was doing fine. I never told anyone just how badly September 11th had affected me. I had led them to believe that things in my life were in order though the reality was much different.

The friends that I talked to on a regular basis never knew of my financial despair either. I continued to make appearances at restaurants and parties when I could. It helped keep my smoke screen intact. Being thirty thousand dollars in debt without a dollar to my name had me teetering on the seesaw of depression. My friends drove nice cars and had houses and talked about retirement. I regaled them with stories of flying and tales from the places I had been. Deep down, I envied them for their stable lives. I wasn't working so that I could enjoy life. Life was making me work to pay a debt and was no longer a pleasure. Many men had jumped off bridges as a solution to the kind of problem I was living through. I was stronger than that, but deep down I knew something had to change; even the strongest have a breaking point.

I dreaded returning home from the Arctic. Those six weeks were the escape from reality that I desperately needed. Sitting around in my empty, run-down apartment made me feel sorry for myself. I didn't have cable television and I had watched every video that I owned at least ten times. I had been home less than a week when my employer called, telling me to pack another suitcase. I was headed to North Carolina for a night vision goggle (NVG) adventure. I pulled a fast break on everything that was depressing me and joined the team that descended on Carolina Country.

Flying at night with NVG's at one hundred and fifty mph just above the treetops is an incredible rush. I really enjoyed the night operations. The guys that I flew with were really fun to be around. We laughed and joked continuously when we were on the ground refueling or refilling the chemical tanks. The company always had food waiting for us too. Hot chocolate, soup, chips and dip, sandwiches, etc. It was more like a family outing than a job.

The first few days went as scheduled, but when we moved north into the Norfolk, Virginia area I thought I had flown my last flight. That's how fast things can change in the world of flying. One minute I was the cocky guy who could do no wrong and the next I was a scared little boy wondering if this job was for me.

We had been spraying directly over the city of Norfolk. I was working the computers and looking out of the cockpit while the other pilot was at the controls. We were having fun dodging the ship's outstretched masts in the harbor as we finished the course line. He banked the plane into a 45-degree turn.

"Do you see it?" I called out.

"Yeah I got it at eleven o'clock," he replied referring to the obstacle in our path. As we moved further into the survey block, our course took us a bit to the southwest and away from the city. The night vision goggles lit the empty hole of darkness as we dive bombed onto the new course line.

"Keep your eyes out for that big antenna over to your left. Do you see it?" I asked.

"There are a couple of them over there and some aren't lit," he answered. An unlit radio tower wasn't easy to spot.

"Do you see that one at twelve o'clock? It's unlit, better go left or right," I told him. I was doing my best looking ahead to make sure our flight path was clear.

"I got it, let's go right," he agreed and turned the plane a few degrees as the unlit tower came into clear view in the goggle's light. We were almost finished for the night. Thirty minutes to completion and then we'd be sitting in a restaurant eating dinner. The last thirty minutes. Anyone in aviation will tell you that the last thirty minutes is where everything goes sour. It's the same as being in a car accident five miles from your house. As the plane turned, my field of vision suddenly became cluttered with towers.

"Watch it another one straight ahead!" I shouted.

"Got it!" he hollered back. "I'm coming to the right some more." As he did, I could see three unlit towers in the luminescent light of the goggles right at our altitude dead ahead. We were almost on top of them!

"PULL UP, PULL UP," I screamed into the microphone. Without hesitation, the aircraft nose went to the sky above us and my eyes were fixated on the stars that were now in my front window. I was envisioning antennas ripping into the hull of the craft and splitting the ship in two. We would surely embrace our mutual fate from opposite sides. I waited for an impact, but nothing. No thud or sound of tearing metal. I stared into the dark as we continued to climb to safety. It was the classic aviation aphorism: "Hours of boredom followed by seconds of sheer terror."

"Did we hit?" he asked. I was speechless. He knew by my silence that we had come far too close. I would guess that we came within ten feet of hitting the antennas. We finished the night at an altitude of five hundred feet agreeing that for safety reasons, it was in our best interest.

After the confidence-shaking night operation, I returned to the Arctic, but to my dismay, I didn't go back to the comfortable confines of Iglulik. I ended up in a mining camp named Lupin located just inside the Arctic Circle in Nunavut. It was an hour and a half flight to the northeast of Yellowknife.

I was originally scheduled to catch a flight from Washington's Dulles Airport connecting in Toronto, then to Edmonton where I would connect to a final flight to take me to Yellowknife. A trip to the Arctic is a tiresome two-day journey. Yellowknife is where I would pick up the 'Diamond Hunter' and fly to Lupin.

The first of a series of belly flops began in Washington when the airline changed the departure gate. I never heard the announcement and consequently missed the flight. The airline put me on a flight to Minneapolis connecting to another to Edmonton. It sounded like a great plan when they laid it out before me. General Custer had a great plan too.

I arrived in Edmonton on the last flight in and found myself being the last person standing around the luggage carousel waiting for bags that never showed. I walked over to the customs agent and after thirty minutes of harassment, I found myself sitting in the office of immigration. I was trying to explain to them that I was only going to be there for a short period of time. They were trying to explain to me that I needed a work permit. By the time we agreed on anything, I had missed my connecting flight to Yellowknife and spent the night in Edmonton.

When I showed up at the ticket counter the next morning, my luggage was waiting for me. The flight to Yellowknife was uneventful, but the weather was beginning to transform into the Arctic weather that I had always read about. The cold was harsh, snow was falling and the winds were gusting. I elected to stay another night in Yellowknife because the weather in Lupin was deteriorating and forecasted to get worse. I spent the afternoon taking in the sights of which there were few.

The following day brought better weather in the morning hours. The forecast for Lupin was afternoon snow showers and low ceilings. I wasn't concerned because I was getting an early start. After I had my gear loaded and just before I closed the door, those beloved Canadian customs agents greeted me once again. What was the problem this time? I knew my paperwork was in order from the dance that I had to do in Edmonton, but they were now requesting to see import papers on the airplane. Evidently, unbeknownst to me, there was an import tax or fee levied against the plane when it was brought across the border. The customs agents had now assumed possession of my plane until the tax was paid.

The total outstanding balance was around forty thousand dollars since they had tracked the airplane's initial entry into the country to when I flew it into Toronto a few months earlier. Terrific. I spent the rest of my morning sitting in the customs office watching the agent drink coffee as fast as the pot could brew it. It was early afternoon before the issue was resolved and I was free to venture out into the Arctic once again.

CHAPTER 20

Return to the Arctic

I wasted no time in launching for my destination. The flight was scheduled for an hour and twenty minutes. By now, the weather in Lupin was below minimums for the approach, but conditions at Yellowknife weren't any better. I knew the client, who was waiting in Lupin, was eager to finish the project and if I had waited for better weather, the job would have been delayed by another week. The snow was already falling and the winds were ripping at thirty knots. I called ahead to the airport meteorologist.

"What's the weather doing?" I asked.

"It's showing three-quarter mile visibility and about 400 overcast," he replied.

"Are you going to try it, eh?" he asked. We both knew that it was well below legal minimums to shoot the approach, but this was Lupin. There weren't any rules in the Arctic.

"I'm coming in," I answered.

"Give me a call ten miles out," he requested.

At the ten-mile mark, I couldn't see the ground due to low clouds and fog and the snowfall made my forward visibility non-existent. The plane was configured to fly the approach. The legal minimum altitude that I could fly the approach down to was five hundred feet and it called for a visibility of one and a half miles, but the overcast was already lower than that with the visibility next to nothing. I set the audible alarm for three hundred feet, though I was fully prepared to fly the craft as low as two hundred. If I didn't see a runway by then, I would be going back to Yellowknife even though the weather there was probably the same.

I radioed in. The weather was now three hundred feet and reporting three-quarter mile visibility. I took a deep breath and held my hand up to the air vent to dry my suddenly sweaty palms. If I had been anywhere else in the world with better options, I wouldn't have attempted the approach, but my alternatives were few. I didn't want to go back to Yellowknife.

I descended to five hundred feet and slowed the aircraft to the final approach speed. I was getting glimpses of the ground and I could tell that the low cloud layer was very thin and had nestled itself over Lupin and only Lupin. At five miles out, I was in the fog solidly with snow pelting the window. I descended to four hundred then to three hundred. I silenced the altimeter's alarm and continued the descent to two hundred feet. The conditions were near white out. I squinted to see the lights, but as I continued to descend, I realized that the lights weren't leading me to the middle of the runway. They were edge lights and the plane was straddling the very edge of the landing strip! To the left of the runway lay a six-foot drop off! If I landed at this very moment, they would be pulling my lifeless corpse from a smoldering heap of metal. I steered the plane to the right to get back on the centerline. I was a few feet off the ground with the nose pointed to one side to correct for the wind when I saw the runway coming up to meet the plane and I immediately stepped on the rudder to straighten the nose. The wheels kissed the ice-covered gravel, but with my rudder correction, the plane began skidding to one side. I played footsies with the rudder pedals, but nothing I did was helping the situation. The nose sashayed left then right and back to the left! I was fishtailing down the runway! As a last resort, I eased the throttles into reverse just as the nose came back across the center. Finally, the Diamond Hunter stopped the side-to-side motion and I was back in control.

"Welcome to Lupin," said a voice over the radio.

I stopped on the runway and rubbed my face with both hands. I was too old for this.

Lupin was a gold mine that was no longer profitable for its current owner. It was profitable at one time, but like any mine, the glitter ran out. In its heyday, Lupin had at least five hundred workers at any given time chipping away at the ore that lay beneath the frozen Arctic tundra. The mine was now being kept on life support by twelve guys whose jobs ranged from cooking for those that were here, to checking the facilities buried in the Earth's throat some fifteen hundred meters below. These guys were the skeleton crew who had been tasked with the dubious honor of euthanizing the mine. The company that owned the land, Echo Bay Mines, was faced with the decision to sell the property as is or take it all down piece by piece and return the land to Mother Nature. If the latter was to come to fruition, the mine would be flooded and the Earth would reclaim its rightful possession.

The little map spec that sat in the middle of the Arctic's white world was actually a self-sustaining town of its own. The camp incorporated its own power plant and generated enough electricity to supply a town of five thousand people. There were dormitory buildings like those found on any college campus with enough rooms to house all that worked here. Most of the rooms had satellite TV and private baths.

The dormitory was connected to the main building. The centerpiece here was the cafeteria. It was open twenty four hours a day seven days a week and the menu was endless! Whatever you were hungry for, this place had it. On more than one occasion, I missed dinner because we were flying, but the cook always fixed me a plate and left it sitting on the counter.

Just outside the cafeteria was a common sitting area with tables and couches and a television that was never turned off. This is where the guys drank their coffee and played poker. Next to this, was a recreation room that housed a shuffleboard table and shelves upon shelves of board games. Other amenities included Billiard tables, dartboards, foosball tables, video rental, three basketball courts, badminton, volleyball, floor hockey, weight room, racquetball courts, and Jacuzzi. It was as if the YMCA had found its way to the land of snow and ice. I'm not sure how much time the workers spent enjoying all of this as they worked twelve hour shifts for two weeks straight. That didn't leave much time to enjoy the recreational aspect of Lupin. Echo Bay Mines also had its own airport complete with a sixty four hundred-foot gravel landing strip and a 727 jumbo jet. From what I was told, the guys there made a decent wage.

Even with all of this at my disposal, I was still restless. I could see the boredom and sadness in the eyes of the crewman when I asked them what their plans were when the doors were shut for good. Some talked of going further north to work for another mining company and others said this was their last hurrah. They were going to retire. I was under the impression that this was all they knew; it was all they had ever done, but frankly, I couldn't imagine them doing anything else. They were born and bred for this type of work and although at first glance one would say they were hard as nails, I found the more I talked to them, the more personable they became. They were just like the people I knew from home doing what they had to do to put food on the table.

Darryl had been mining most of his life. Lupin was his last hurrah. The lines on his face told more stories than Darryl himself. He stood about 5'8" and he wore his gray hair in a flat top. He had a hardened look about him. Darryl was in charge of the power plant and even gave me a guided tour, but I usually met up with him around midnight when I was making the long walk to the cafeteria in search of a midnight snack.

He would stand with one leg perched on the heating pipe that was attached to the lower portion of the hallway wall with his elbow resting on elevated knee. He stood there staring out into the Arctic darkness watching the snow invade Lupin under the dim outside lights; his cigarette clinched between his index and middle fingers. He was the coolest smoker I had ever seen and I don't just mean cool; Darryl was 1950s, pack rolled up in your sleeve cool. He could be in the middle of telling you a story when he would pull out a cigarette, light it and then methodically insert it between his lips never taking his eyes off of you. The stories he would tell made me feel like a kid hiding behind the couch while the adults talked after a holiday meal. His thick Canadian accent had me hanging on every word. Every question ended with "eh?" Every gesture he made had meaning.

He began all of his stories with some sort of characterization of the antagonist. "Tough guy this guy, eh?" or "Oh this guy was so dumb, eh?" following it up with a look of disbelief and a slow shake of his head.

His greatest story involved him and a friend and a plot to import fish illegally. Darryl's friend was a pilot and he had asked Darryl if he wanted to be a partner in importing fish. He didn't give Darryl the details but it sounded like a good idea. The friend told Darryl that he would fly up to see him and pitch the whole idea in person. Darryl agreed, but after waiting on his friend for hours, he figured he'd been stood up and went about his business. It turned out that the authorities had caught up with the pilot and had taken him into custody. His plane was loaded with fish that he hadn't paid import tax on. He was arrested and jailed for a lengthy stint. It wasn't until months later that the story unfolded and Darryl was made aware of the whereabouts of his buddy.

I was eager to learn about the mine's past and I tried to envision the establishment with the energy of five hundred workers.

"Do you want to go down the shaft, eh?" one of the guys asked.

My heart was pounding at the thought of it and I said, "Let's go." When would I ever have this chance again?

"Come on," he beckoned.

He led me into the safety equipment room at the surface and gave me the required safety brief like a flight attendant at the beginning of a flight. Like those airline speeches, it was more like a rehearsed preamble used to satisfy a regulation rather than anything that would actually help me to survive an emergency.

On top of my head perched a miner's lamp from which dangled a battery pack. I clipped the pack housing to the equipment belt that now hung around my waist. I was fitted and ready to see what lay in the stomach of the earth! I looked at the man lift on the far wall. It was an open elevator that led to the bottom of the mine. I guess now would have been a good time to tell my guide that I was very afraid of heights. Riding a man lift would push me to the limit of my fear. I slowly started to move in the direction of the lift.

"This way," he called out. "We're going to drive down the shaft."

"Oh thank you, thank you, thank you!"

We passed through a doorway and then another and finally into a wide-open equipment bay. There was a snowplow and a few other vehicles that were used to sustain the operation on the surface. As we passed each and every one of them on our way to an immense garage door, we stopped and my guide introduced me to the most rugged jeep pickup truck I had ever seen. It had been modified by the artistic hands of company welders and resembled something out of a Mad Max movie. The truck frame was encased with steel tubing and angel iron.

With the push of a button, the over-sized garage door rolled up and out of sight. The truck carefully ate its way through the snowfall. I strained my eyes to see where we were going. The frozen tundra presented a very uncomfortable ride under the steel-belted treads. We were heading toward the lake when the guide turned us left into what looked like an expansive metal drainage tube. It was befitting that the hole leading me into the depths of Mother Earth looked like an esophagus. He perched the wheels on the edge of the tunnel and looked at me.

"Are you ready?" he asked. He knew my heart was beating out of control. Maybe he was thinking of his first day going down into the mine.

"Ready as I'll ever be!" I exclaimed. He nudged the truck over the edge. It grabbed me like a roller coaster. We were facing down at about thirty degrees and the engine whined as he kept it in low gear. The perma-frost on the shaft wall was two feet thick. We were descending into a deep freezer. I could feel the warm air moving past us making its escape to the atmosphere above. The frosted wall coating lasted nearly twenty-five yards then tapered off to nothing, but the rugged rib bones of the earth. We continued to spiral down the shaft. My guide stopped the vehicle and killed the lights.

"Can you see anything?" he asked. "This is as dark as the world will ever get." He wasn't kidding. I couldn't see my hand an inch from my face. It was eerie to say the least.

We passed tunnels on every side of us. It was a network that to me had no sense of organization. I tried to imagine them filled with monstrous drilling equipment and heavy dirt haulers that moved the earth in search of the precious gold.

We came to rest at what was known as the six fifty shop, appropriately named for being six hundred and fifty meters below the surface. This was as far as the tour was going even though the shaft went as far as fifteen hundred meters.

The air here was different. It was being pumped in from the world above, but somewhere along its route something about it had changed. I couldn't put my finger on it, but my chest felt tight. When we exited the vehicle, my guide starting explaining the process of how the walls and ceilings were reinforced to prevent collapse. It seemed important and very relevant since I stood beneath tons of rock that looked like it was being suspended with chicken wire.

Electrical bundles that fed electricity to the lights and supplied power throughout the underground world hung from the walls and draped down from overhead. The dingy light in there was cast from numerous single bulb outlets that seemed to hold nothing greater than a sixty watt bulb. The six fifty shop was a repair shop for the heavy loaders and dozers and was nothing more than an immense hole cut out of the side of the tunnel. From the back wall to the shop entrance, the heavy loaders lay single filed. They resembled people lining up for an unwanted march. The floor was wet and the walls were bleeding with moisture. So this is what the belly of the planet looked like. I stood and gawked at the intestinal membrane that encompassed me as my ears popped from the mild pressure. I spent thirty minutes down in that hole learning about mining excavations, but by the time we reached the light on the surface again; the only real lesson I came away with was the fact that I could never work in a mine!

Though my purpose at Lupin was to continue the survey operation that had been started months earlier in Iglulik, I wasn't doing any flying. The weather wasn't cooperating at all, which was fine with me; I was shooting hoops, lifting weights, and assembling one thousand-piece puzzles.

The client had metamorphosed into a complete jerk, far from the man who had displayed such a wonderful sense of humor in Iglulik. Most people working in the far north are given one week off every six weeks and sent back to civilization, but this guy had been up here since the inception of the project. It was obviously taking its toll. I certainly sympathized with him as the job was well behind schedule from bad weather and equipment problems. We routinely butted heads when it came to whether we would fly or not. I wasn't about to venture out and get caught in the fog that always settled over Lupin. The client on the other hand, had no concern for safety and he routinely lobbied to fly everyday regardless of weather conditions. If we flew, he was the happiest guy in the world, if we didn't; he wouldn't talk to me and even resorted to sitting at the far end of the cafeteria eating dinner alone. It seemed rather childish, but that's how he preferred it. I found it laughable that two guys in one of the most remote places on earth sat on opposite ends of a cafeteria in complete silence.

The days that we did fly started out with a caveman-like approach to weather forecasting. I had access to a computer, but there wasn't any radar that far north and just as I had been in Iglulik, I was reduced to looking at prognostic charts that were basically useless. In addition to the weather causing delays, we were now faced with much shorter days. We were losing light at the rate of six minutes a day. As it was, the sun was rising at eleven o'clock in the morning and setting at three in the afternoon. One flight a day was all we could manage.

My primitive way of forecasting the weather consisted of me standing in front of the big picture window in the cafeteria and peering out over Lake Contwoyto, which lay to the north of the camp. I would take my thumb and index finger and place them directly in front of my eye. My index finger would lie at the base of the cloud layer as I looked between them and my thumb would rest on the Earth's surface on the other side of the lake. If I had at least an inch of space between my fingers, it equated to a cloud base between seven hundred and a thousand feet above the ground. My method was just as good if not better than the airport meteorologist. He released a balloon and counted how many seconds it took before it disappeared into the cloud cover. We usually came out close to the same number.

The terrain that surrounded Lupin was an Arctic desert. The land was flat and featureless except for the lake. There wasn't any wildlife in these parts except the occasional Arctic hare and fox. It was completely opposite of Iglulik where I had counted no less than thirty polar bears during one flight. Rowley Island in the Foxe Basin was a Polar Bear breeding ground. Caribou herds littered the land on all sides of Iglulik and Beluga Whales frolicked among the icebergs. It was like every National Geographic show I had ever seen, but there was nothing of the sort in Lupin.

After I had diagnosed the weather situation, the next step was to uncover the airplane. It snowed every night and once for six days straight. We kept a space heater in the plane to keep the instrumentation from freezing. It kept the temperature at about ten degrees. Though the airplane was always mechanically sound, the brakes did freeze up often, which made the taxi downhill to the runway rather unnerving.

The best thing about the flying in Lupin was that the survey block was never really too far away. The problem was that the weather was seldom flyable. Lake Contwoyto was constantly producing fog that made it impossible to get back into Lupin. The flat white terrain coupled with never ending snow showers made for complete white out conditions. The few days that I was able to fly took a tremendous amount of planning.

The take off sequence alone was hair-raising! The runway was elevated above the surrounding land, which put the earth's surface at the end of the runway roughly one hundred and fifty feet below it. It wasn't a straight drop off, but more of a sloping grade. When the plane lifted off, I had to pull the power back and push forward on the controls to level the craft at fifty feet, then, as I crossed over the end of the runway, I would dive down following the sloping terrain and level off at one hundred feet above the lake. I would fly at this altitude until we reached the survey block. This procedure kept me out of the cloud base and was my best option to maintain good visibility. I had two alternate airports that were both less than an hour away, but both rested on the shore of a body of water, which meant that the weather at either of those would be the same as Lupin.

The two weeks I spent in Lupin seemed like two months. I passed most of my time watching snowflakes fall from the big picture window in the cafeteria. When it came time to leave, the best weather that Mother Nature could provide appeared in the wee hours of the morning. Snow was falling and the wind was howling as the temperature reached a minus thirty. As I passed through the double doors that separated the mudroom from the harsh arctic environment, I smiled and read the words on a chart: "Skin freezes at this temperature." It was a reminder of where in the world I was.

When I turned onto the runway for my final departure from Lupin, I was hit with the conviction that everyone should get the chance to experience this part of the world at least once in their lifetime. I pushed the throttles forward and roared down the snow-covered strip. As I pulled back on the yoke, the plane leaped into the sky and plunged head first into the cloud deck. She wasn't there long before I shot out of the top into the star field that cluttered the darkness. As I checked my instruments, I could see that a few of them had become casualties of the bitter cold. I didn't care. I had enough working on the panel to get to Yellowknife. I threw the ship into a hard left bank, a bank of confidence and one that you don't do with passengers on board. I had the wings vertical to the world below and as I rolled out of the turn, an apparition danced its way across the sky directly in front of me. The Northern Lights. I was mesmerized. A grin lit across my face. This was why I had wanted to fly; for these once-in-a-lifetime moments.

CHAPTER 21

Safety Concerns

I boarded a commercial flight in Yellowknife and spent the night in the great city of Toronto before continuing home. There I was able to partake in the wonderful food and spirits that Toronto certainly offers. It was the welcome back to civilization that I needed.

By the time I arrived in Virginia, however, my mood was a somber one. I had just been to a place where few had, and now I would have to readjust to the ways of small town America. The company didn't have me scheduled for another project until January. In the interim, I would be working in the maintenance shop. It was a cruel transition going from being my own boss and working a short four hour day to being under the control of an eight hour time clock. Thankfully, I was placed in the company of guys who made the work day fun. They helped me to get through the next three weeks until my next project, the Texas Rabies Vaccination Program or TRV.

The company sent four planes and a handful of pilots to conquer the southern border between Texas and Mexico. Had it not been for a line drawn in bold black ink on my map, I would have never been able to tell the two apart. Southern Texas is the third world of North America. It was littered with small towns that offer nothing more than a dense population of trailers and junked vehicles scattered among the desert cactus. Pilots who had this job in previous years raved that this project was one of the most enjoyable that they had ever been on. As a result of this exaltation, I questioned their sanity.

Finding a decent restaurant to eat in became a chore. Every other building was a Mexican restaurant. It took all of two days before my body succumbed to the dysentery that was so common in Mexico. Not that I drank the water in the border towns of southern Texas; as far as I was concerned, it was just northern Mexico. The only two cities that I would classify as American were Laredo and Brownsville, but unfortunately I only saw them from the sky. I spent the majority of my off time in places like Zapata, Fort Stockton, and Junction, not to mention Mexia (pronounced Ma-hey-a), which has the dubious honor of being the former home to the one and only Anna Nicole Smith.

The TRV mission was simple. Eradicate and continually monitor the eradication of the rabies virus in the state of Texas. Rabies outbreaks in the state are rare; however, it is virtually impossible to stop rabid animals in Mexico from wandering across the border. Frankly, if we haven't figured out how to stop twelve million illegal aliens from crossing the border, we certainly wouldn't be able to thwart the efforts of a sick coyote.

The method used to control and eradicate the virus was ingenious in its simplicity. Someone designed a small square block made of pressed fishmeal and in the center of the block was a packet containing a rabies vaccination. Inside the airplane was a machine that held hundreds of these blocks and dropped them out of the bottom of the plane as we flew.

The TRV operation was seriously flawed, however, when it came to respecting the limits of safety. Management had little concern for the safety of the pilots involved. They were more concerned with meeting the deadline of the project. Both TRV management and the company that I worked for were continually pushing us into situations that forced us to break federally mandated rules. The bottom line here was that they had us under their thumb because if we didn't fly, we didn't get paid.

Ignorance and arrogance are two things that will get you killed in aviation. If you tell someone that you aren't going to fly because the weather is bad or the plane isn't mechanically sound, there is always some arrogant idiot who will step in and fly the plane regardless of the rules being broken and the safety being compromised. We were flying in severe turbulence at five hundred feet above the terrain and on one occasion we flew with the wind at the airport reaching speeds in excess of forty miles per hour, which was well beyond the structural limit for the plane. We routinely launched airplanes that were covered with frost. The problem being that frost on a wing diminishes the lift producing capability of the wing, making it very difficult for the airplane to become airborne. More importantly, it's I-L-L-E-G-A-L according to federal regulations. If there had been an FAA representative on site, every pilot there would have lost his license. We flew in dust storms that brought visibility to a mile and we flew airplanes with known mechanical problems. Both of which are illegal. One of the planes that I flew had an inoperative fuel transfer pump. We had a new part to repair it and willing mechanics to do the work, but management refused. I remember taxiing to the runway behind another plane. The guy piloting that plane radioed in saying he thought he kicked up some rocks into his propeller. "We'll check it out when you get back," was the reply. When he returned, he was startled to see that the propeller blade had a tear in the metal that was at least three-quarters of an inch deep. The tear was well beyond repairable limits. Legally it would require a new propeller blade to return the plane to mechanical soundness, but management refused to repair it.

I started to voice my opinion on the lack of safety concerns. The company's solution to that was to remove me from TRV. They sent me to Mexia to perform periodic maintenance inspections on some of the planes. I knew I was being sent simply because they were tired of me not because I had some unbelievable mechanical skill above and beyond that of the other guys. I found it comical when they brought the airplane with the cracked propeller in for its inspection. The inspector took one look at it and shook his head.

"I know you don't think I'm going to pass that!" he exclaimed. "I can't believe you flew it in here like that." Little did he know they had been flying it all week!

I stayed in Mexia for four days. Turning wrenches instead of flying meant a four-dollar an hour pay cut. My departure from the flight operation satisfied the company management as well as those at TRV. The guy in charge of TRV was not a bit pleased with me voicing my concerns for safety. If we followed the rules, the project wouldn't make the deadline. This guy had no knowledge of aviation or the rules that governed it; yet, he was telling me when it was and was not safe to launch my airplane. This represented what I had been saying all along in regards to the pilots' managers. They were "yes" men through and through. They had no backbones and because of it, we continued to fly in unsafe hazardous conditions. The other pilots complained to me and I complained out loud, which made me the fall guy. The head of TRV even told my employer that he took great offense to me calling the rabies bait blocks "coyote cookies" and "fox fritters." He said that I was poking fun at the program. I already stated that I thought it was ingenious, but the way he ran the program would have resulted in us being shut down had the FAA been on site.

TRV came and went and I found myself ferrying company airplanes from storage in Oklahoma to Texas and Virginia. This was also some of the most imprudent flying known to man. It consisted of retrieving airplanes that had been in storage for a lengthy period of time and flying them to a place where overhaul maintenance would return them to airworthy status. Most of the planes had only three instruments in the panel and it was common practice to install a box in the right seat that contained a GPS, a radio, and a transponder, which allowed ATC to locate the plane on radar. After a brief systems check, we would launch into the sky literally on a "wing and a prayer."

On one of these flights, I was forced to land in Kentucky due to an engine problem. As I sat and waited for a company mechanic to come out and assess the problem, I was reading the paperwork that gave me authorization from the FAA to fly an airplane in such a condition. Yes it is legal, but not very smart and truth be known, the FAA doesn't really know the condition of the airplane. They don't come out and look at it before you fly. The judgment is left up to the pilot and my paycheck had certainly clouded my judgment. As I continued to read the paperwork out of sheer boredom, I came across a sentence in big, bold, black letters. NO CARGO IS TO BE CARRIED. It was plain as day. The back of my plane was filled with aircraft parts from storage. Technically, it was cargo. Would the FAA ever find out? No, but this is a situation where pilots get themselves into deep water with the authorities. What if I had to declare an emergency due to my engine trouble? That would require the FAA to show up on site and investigate, which would reveal the violation. Who gets punished for the infraction? The pilot. I worked too hard to achieve my licenses to have them snatched away because my employer blatantly didn't care. I picked up the phone and gave an earful to a manager back in Virginia. He gave me an excuse that technically it wasn't cargo and blah blah blah. I flew the crippled plane back to Virginia driven by sheer anger.

I was, at that time, talking to a prospective employer about life after the ridiculously unsafe and unregulated flying that I was currently doing. I was still climbing the career ladder trying to land that first jet job. My good friend Pete from my days in Petersburg had become part of a management team that was in the process of starting a company flying jets out of Roanoke, Virginia. Pete told me over the phone that I was hired, but the new company wouldn't be able to send me to school for at least two maybe three months. I told him that I would stay put for the time being, but assured him that when he called, I would be ready to go. Deep down I knew the jet job was exactly what my résumé needed, but I was resenting the fact that I would have to relocate. It would be the fourth time in two years.

During each move, I threw out anything that I hadn't used in the past few months. I was preparing for the next inevitable move long before it happened. I was currently driving a ten-year old pick-up truck that helped to better facilitate each relocation. My household goods consisted of a bed, a TV, and kitchen utensils. The rest of my life was still in boxes that hadn't been touched since I left American Airlines. I had become a traveling showman and a modern day gypsy without ever intending to. All that was missing was a top hat and a box of snake oil.

In addition to the hassles of relocating, I was going to have to take another pay cut. That would mean that since my departure from American a short two and a half years earlier, I would have cut my yearly income by fifty thousand dollars. This was not a good idea since I was thirty thousand in the hole. Though I was slowly progressing with my flying career, the decision to change careers after the age of thirty was looking like it had been a bad one. I continued to give the impression that life was just peachy when I talked to people back home, but the weight of the financial strain was taking its toll. I was barely making enough money to keep my head above water and the thought of taking another decrease in salary kept me in a state of depression. My current job was exciting, but being over the age of thirty meant that I was wise enough to know that the longer I stayed, the greater chance I had of losing my license or worse, my life, simply because of the lack of safety in the operation.

CHAPTER 22

Haiti

After the unpleasant trip to Texas with the TRV project, I was absolutely delighted when I was told to pack a suitcase and return to Canada. I was going to Toronto. I would gladly work there seven days a week and twice on Sunday. The assignment was the easiest to date. A client was developing and testing laser equipment that could map the land under water. It gave hope to doing away with some of the tasks that were assigned to basic sonar. The fact that the technology was in its infantile stages of development meant that there was very little flying. I ventured out over Lake Ontario one hundred feet above the water while the client fiddled with and cussed at his equipment.

"We're going to have to go back," he told me. I could see the disappointment in his eyes. "It's going to take a day or two to get this thing figured out. I'll call you when we're ready to try it again."

"I'll be at the hotel," I told him. After that, I went out to enjoy Toronto's nightlife. First stop? Chinatown. I was hardly concerned that I wasn't making any money due to the fact that I wasn't flying. Emotionally, I was on the border of depression and Toronto was precisely what I needed to fix what ailed me.

The following day I received a call at the hotel. I thought it was the client calling to say he had sorted out the problems. To my surprise, it was a manager from the home office.

"How's the job going up there?" he asked.

"It's going to be a long drawn out ordeal," I answered. "They've got equipment problems."

"Those guys are famous for that," he laughed. "Listen, we need someone to go into Haiti to work with the State Department. We prefer someone with your background. Interested?"

I had just switched on CNN and saw that Haiti was in a state of turmoil bordering on civil war. The current president Jean Bertrand Aristide was being evicted from power and angry Haitians were ravaging the country.

"Did you ask anybody else to do it?" I asked. I wanted to know if I was their only option in the hopes of negotiating some sort of hazardous duty pay.

"Not yet," was the reply.

"Let me think about it and I'll call you back." I hung up the phone then immediately called another pilot who I thought might know more about the mission. I skipped over the basic pleasantries.

"Did they call you?" I asked. He knew immediately who it was. Michael was another go-to guy for the company. If the company had something out of the norm, it was guys like us that received the call. Most of his experience was in Central

America residing in the country of Panama and flying in and out of Mexico.

"About twenty minutes ago," he replied.

"They told me that they hadn't offered it to anyone yet," I laughed. "How stupid do they think I am? Are you going to take it?" I continued.

"That place is a war zone. If they want me for the job, it's going to cost them seventy five thousand dollars, and you know they won't pay it," he answered.

"Did you tell them that?" I asked.

"That's why they called you."

"What about Phil?" I continued. Phil was another any time any place kind of guy.

"He said the same thing. Walk away from it man; you're liable to get killed down there. They're not going to pay you what's right, guaranteed. They've got bodies in the streets, riots, shootings, it's not worth it," he finished.

I needed the extra money that might come with this job. I was a mercenary at this point not concerned about the dangers. I was chasing the almighty dollar.

"I'll let you know what I decide," I told him then hung up the phone. I called operations. "I'll do it for extra cash," I stated right out of the box.

"We're working on that right now," he said. It was bold, hard-nosed negotiating that stood between ops and my taking the assignment. I was their third choice and probably their final option so I figured I had the upper hand.

"What about firearms?" I asked.

"I can't authorize it," he said as if that was something that wasn't even a remote possibility.

"You want me to go into a war zone empty handed?" I asked in disbelief. "You're not asking much are you?"

"I've got my hands tied over here. If something goes wrong, then we've got an international incident on our hands," he replied. "Listen, you're going to be operating out of Port Au Prince. The Marines are heading in right now to secure the airfield and Canada is sending troops as well," trying to reassure me that this was just another assignment.

"Who or what will I be flying?" I inquired.

"State Department folks, French dignitaries, and possibly some evacuation flights to the DR." The DR was the Dominican Republic. It was night and day difference between the two countries where infrastructure and government were concerned. The DR was civil, business as usual, while Haiti was in the early stages of an uprising and the only person that represented the presence of governmental control had just fled the country.

"We need to get you on a plane ASAP," he continued. "We'll bring you home so you can pick up the plane here. We've got to have you in Palm Beach tonight, and then tomorrow you'll be flying down to Haiti with a guy from AirServ. He'll be the liaison between you and the State Department. They do this kind of thing all the time." Again trying to smooth the rough edges on a hostile mission.

AirServ. I knew a little bit about their background and purpose. They had been in every country on the planet and they specialized in working for organizations like the State Department. It bolstered my confidence and calmed my nerves.

I boarded a flight at Toronto's International Airport bound for Washington D.C. There, I grabbed a rental car and made the two hour drive to company headquarters. By now it was ten o'clock at night and I was tired. My plane sat on the ramp. I opened the door and tossed my gear inside.

"You ready for this?" I asked the hunk of metal as I climbed in. I had already been reassured that the plane had been preflighted by the chief pilot in order to expedite my departure. Let me give the pilots out there a piece of advice. If someone tells you that your airplane has already been checked and that it's good to go, preflight it again with a fine tooth comb!

I was having a profoundly difficult time understanding why I had to have the plane in Palm Beach that night. I could have left early in the morning and been there before noon. I had been awake since 7:00 a.m., which meant that I was well beyond any fourteen-hour day. That's the amount of hours in a day that I could legally be expected to remain on duty. I had pleaded my case to management before I boarded the plane to Washington. We weren't saving any time or even getting a head start by having me fly down in the middle of the night.

I jumped into the cockpit and began to get situated when I noticed the charts that the chief pilot had placed in the plane were well out of date. This would cost me another thirty-minute delay while I located legal charts. I was beginning to think that Barnum and Bailey were in charge of this operation. When I finally thought that things were in enough order to take to the skies, I launched out into a partially clouded night.

I had been in the air no more than ten minutes when I found myself in the middle of an overcast. No biggie, but since I was tired, I decided to let the autopilot fly it. I reached down to engage it and nothing happened. I tried several times to no avail. Now I found myself searching for circuit breakers and loose wires trying to solve the issue in the dark. I shook my head in disgust for the guy who supposedly did the preflight as I knew then that no one had really looked the plane over. My first instinct was to turn around and go home, but a cooler temper finally prevailed. "I sure wish Pete would get things up and running with the jets," I said to myself. It was time to move on.

I hand flew the plane for the three hour trip to Palm Beach. The enroute weather had me flying in and out of storms, but the destination weather was good so the landing sequence was uneventful. I grabbed my things and headed to the hotel because I knew I had to be up early.

Ring! I grabbed it before the second ring.

"Hello?"

"You up?" he asked. It was a company manager who was also going to be the second pilot. I was the only one that they had convinced to take the job so management had to take an active role.

"I'm up," I said. I had been glued to CNN's coverage of the crisis in Haiti.

"We're going to meet for breakfast at eight," he informed me. "Why don't you meet us?"

"Ok," I replied. It was 7:45 a.m. I brushed my teeth and threw on the same clothes from the night before. I checked the television again to see if anything was new and improved in Haiti. New? Yes. Improved? Not even close.

"Morning, Gentlemen!" It was my best attempt at disguising my foul mood from the events of the previous night.

"Good Morning!" they replied in unison. They didn't need a disguise since they had flown in at their leisure the previous day. The company manager sat next to the AirServ representative that I had been expecting. He laid out the whole mission from start to finish. We would be flying whatever or whomever the U.S. State Department wanted us to. We were contractors for them; war gophers with absolutely no care or concern for the plight of the Haitian people. We were figures of neutrality in a country of opposing sides. I sure hoped that someone had told that to the rebels.

"So what time do we launch?" I asked. The formalities were over.

"Sometime tomorrow, we still don't have the State Department's authorization to enter the country," he answered.

"Oh, really?" I questioned in a tone that was slowly heating to a boiling point.

I ate my breakfast in hurried fashion and remained silent throughout. "I'm going out to the plane this morning to fix my autopilot," I stated as a matter of fact and excused myself. I was furious to find out that I didn't really need to be here yet.

I drove to the airfield to investigate the faulty autopilot. The company manager caught up to me at the plane.

"What's the matter with the autopilot?" he asked

"I don't know. Won't engage."

"You mad at me?"

"No," I answered. I then commenced to tell the story of the events from the day before culminating with the faulty autopilot. I told him that I had had enough of the lies from management.

"Let me fix this and you go get some sleep," he offered.

"I'm alright. I just needed to vent. I'll get over it," I assured him. "So what's your take on this thing? Haiti, I mean."

"Not sure, but I'm sure we'll be fine," he said.

I looked around the tarmac. Planes of all types were loading up with emergency supplies waiting for the "all clear" so they could swarm into the little Caribbean island country all in the name of good faith. Ninety miles off the coast of Florida yet far removed from any resemblance of civilization.

"I found your problem!" he exclaimed.

"What's that?" I asked.

"They never hooked up the control box. There's the plug right there," he confirmed. I just shook my head as I turned away. I was going to take him up on the offer to return to the hotel and sleep.

I woke up bright and early and started the day without breakfast. We had our authorization from the State Department, which gave us the green light to launch. I taxied out following my comrades. We had discussed our plans and the role we would fulfill, but no matter how concrete it sounded it was only a bowlful of speculation.

The weather was beautiful for the flight. As the tower cleared me for takeoff, he asked, "Going down full and coming back empty?"

"Going full and staying," I replied.

"Oh," he stated. I guess that sounded a little crazy to him. The airport had been launching planes of all different types headed to Haiti that day, but most would be returning by nightfall. His reply summed up the way I felt; nervous and unsure.

"You're cleared for takeoff. Runway heading to five thousand."

As I left the safety of the Florida coast, I was intoxicated by the magnificence of the Caribbean waters. The Bahamas were off to my left and Greater Inagua was directly in my path. It was only a scattered layer of clouds that infrequently cluttered my view. The airplane was flying flawlessly on its recently repaired autopilot.

The flight lasted two and a half hours before I entered into Haitian airspace. I made the turn west to join the final approach corridor into Port Au Prince. Smoke filled the skies. From where I sat, it looked like a war zone. The air that entered the aircraft's ventilation system smelled like a war zone. As I crossed short final, I could see that the Marines were settling in on airport grounds.

We deplaned only to find no one in the customs office. We strolled through the stark terminal building. The masses were on the outside at the main entrance trying to gain entry in the hopes of catching a flight to anywhere. This was the safest place in Port Au Prince, which didn't bolster my confidence since we would soon be leaving this post.

Our AirServ rep had secured the services of a local driver named DeVaulier who would chauffer us back and forth from the airport to the safe house. He loaded our bags and two more people for a total of five into a shell of a metal box better suited for the refuse bin than the road. The heat was exhausting and the vehicle was without air conditioning. It was also devoid of carpet, radio and comfort. We bumbled our way onto the main thoroughfare outside the airport. Here, life looked normal albeit flaunting third world looks with dilapidated houses and inner city charm. We drove a half-mile to a roundabout and that's where everything changed. Vehicles were turned over on their sides and engulfed in flames. Local inhabitants were screaming and shouting in favor of a cause. Smoke made me gag as we sped past the riotous scene. I quickly removed my pilot bars from my shoulders. In a country that was richly impoverished, I didn't want to be the one looking like I had an education and money.

We drove onto the main road that would lead us into the heart of the city. Monstrous burning trash mounds lined the street and at some points they forced the four-lane road into two. Pigs and chickens and grotesquely thin dogs wandered about. Some of the locals embraced the façade that it was business as usual as they walked with laundry perched upon their heads. Children followed close behind with the day's water carried in the same manner. Our driver opted to leave the main road in the interest of saving time.

The side street was an ignored stretch of dirt and rock studded with deep ruts that rocked the Toyota mercilessly. We had to drive down the middle to avoid the worst of the road's hazards, which forced us to meander around oncoming (albeit slowly moving) traffic. Eventually, we found ourselves back on pavement sneaking up on the backside of an area of town called Petionville.

This part of town was home to open markets and a central bus stop both of which lay directly in our path. It was Haiti's Grand Central Station. The vehicle slowed to a crawl again and stopped frequently. Thousands of Haitians had spilled into the street blocking our route. The Toyota's horn blared unnoticed. I tried to remain calm, but I'm sure my nervousness showed.

The house was the second to last at the end of a dead end road. It was one of a handful that rested off the road protected by concrete walls and iron gates. The tops of the walls were implanted with broken chards of glass to deter would-be thieves. The entrance gate resembled a jail cell door.

I grabbed my gear and settled into a room upstairs at the back of the house. I then ventured out into the street and followed it to the dead end. The road came to a close at the edge of a cliff that looked down into a valley. Shacks and shanties built on top of each other dotted the land below. The inhabitants seemed oblivious to the political upheaval as they went about their daily chores. I went back into the house and joined my comrades at the dinner table.

After the evening meal, I retired upstairs in the hopes of taking a shower. The bathroom was in shambles. Not quite as bad as what I had dealt with in Iglulik, but certainly not up to my standards. I had to perform maintenance on the toilet in order to get it to flush and the best I could do for a stream of water was a trickle. I managed to wash the filth off my body with the use of a wash towel and a cup. Even though the day had been exhausting, sleep was hard to come by as machine gun fire and shotgun blasts sounded throughout the night.

The itinerant roosters that roamed the streets and yards first witnessed the morning light. I went downstairs and clambered into the worn out Toyota with the others. Our driver met us with a big smile and a hearty "Good Morning!" Haiti was awakening. The markets were preparing for the day's business and masses of children walked to school dressed in the familiar plaid that symbolized the pursuit of a religious education. Where was the war?

The Marines had settled on the far side of the airfield and the Canadian troops had begun setting up camp less than fifty yards from where my plane was parked. The airport was open for business, but the commercial airlines had suspended service so the only planes destined for Haiti were cargo planes and international aid transports. Haitians continued to line up outside the terminal in the hopes of getting on board a flight leaving the turmoil, but without commercial service they wouldn't have any luck.

I began planning my flight to Port de Paix. The only information I had was the longitude and latitude coordinates until one of the local pilots volunteered some valuable counsel.

"Port de Paix? I've been there," he stated. "Four thousand feet of gravel and nasty, nasty winds. I think the runways are nine and two-seven or close to it. You land nine and you take off nine." He grabbed a napkin and began to draw me a map. "There are houses over here and here, the parking area is here. They used to fly a dash seven in there so it's plenty wide enough. Hop over this mountain," he pointed north, "then snake through the valley, just follow the river, it'll lead you in the right direction. At the end of the valley on the north end, you'll see what looks like a beach, turn for it. Then, you'll see a fence here," again pointing and drawing. "You'll see a bunch of laundry on the fence, runway nine, or whatever it is, is just on the other side of it. Good luck."

I loaded up seven French ambassadors for the twenty-five minute flight to the north side of the island. Twenty-five minutes could get you anywhere in Haiti by plane.

We launched out over the mountain range climbing to fifty five hundred feet. I slipped between clouds that were at six thousand and mountaintops that were close to five thousand. Once on the other side, I was out of Port Au Prince's airspace meaning I was on my own. I scaled down the mountain slope and traversed the valley over the river at two thousand feet. The visibility was good beneath the clouds and the valley presented a magnificent view that was equal to a thunderstorm passing over a Texas prairie. I could see the virga dangling from beneath the dark ominous clouds and light rain danced on my windshield. I zigzagged between the rain showers keeping my distance from the mountain's edge. The flight was very turbulent, yet manageable. I was overcome with the same adrenaline rush I had experienced in the Arctic.

The valley at the north end began to bottleneck and forced me under the rain clouds reducing my visibility. I could smell the tropical rain coming through the vents. I bullied my way through the it and came face to face with the sand bar that the local pilot had referred to as a beach. I looked at the napkin map to reassure myself. The winds had suddenly grown violent, as there was nothing between the ocean and me. The craft shook impetuously. The "laundry fence" came into view as I struggled to control the plane. I turned for the fence and looked at my compass. It was runway nine just like he had said. I firmly planted the airplane on the gravel strip and turned into the parking area. The children stood on the walls that surrounded the runway. They smiled and waved oblivious to our reasons for being there.

I followed my seven passengers as they waded into a sea of Haitians. The man in charge turned to me and very calmly said, "It's not safe for you to stay here, go on back to Port Au Prince. We'll be ready at three o'clock."

He didn't have to tell me twice. I turned around and made my way back through the freshly cut path. I jumped into the plane, which was now surrounded by locals and strapped myself into the seat. I gave a quick look to see that no one was in danger of being hit by a spinning propeller and started one engine. As I began to taxi, people moved from around the plane and took up positions on the runway edge. I started the second engine on the roll. I taxied to the start of runway nine and made a one eighty -degree turn to face the direction of my departure. I looked down the runway to assess its condition. Deep ruts and large rocks were strewn in my path. Townspeople were milling about at the far end of the strip. I pushed the throttles forward, but held the brakes in an effort to let them know to get out of the way and in doing so gave the clean laundry on the fence a dusting of dirt and pebbles. I gave the ladies an apologetic glance and let go of the brakes. The wingtips barely cleared the heads of those that stood on the outskirts. Those at the far end only turned their heads in my direction when I sucked the wheels up and turned out over the ocean to the left. The plane rocked violently as I climbed above the clouds in search of a smooth ride back to Port Au Prince.

I was learning to adjust to being in Haiti. I had acclimated myself to dribble showers, but no matter how much effort I put forth, the sounds of gunfire at bedtime never seemed ordinary. In fact, one night during the first week of our stay, I was awakened to the sound of a gun battle on the street in front of our concrete fortress. BOOM! I leapt out of bed and onto the floor. At first, I thought that the iron gates had been breached. I scurried to the end of the bed and wedged myself between the bed and the wall just beneath the window looking into the courtyard. I began contemplating my options had rebels actually penetrated the security of the building. BOOM! A second time. I guessed the assailant was ten feet in front of the house.

"Are you ok over there?" I called to the other pilot across the courtyard.

"I'm alright. Can you see anything?" he asked.

"Nothing. It's pitch black," I replied. I waited for something other than silence as I huddled in my current position for the remainder of the night and praised the rooster call at first light.

Our commutes to and from the airfield gave us interesting views into everyday life in Haiti. As I sat in the back of chauffer DeVaulier's beastly machine hemmed in by the hustle and bustle of Petionville, I noticed a man walking down the sidewalk stark naked except for a hat on his head.

"Hellooo, naked man at 3 o'clock!" I cried out.

"What? Where?" they cried.

"Over there!" I pointed. The car erupted with laughter as DeVaulier told us that this particular man lived nearby and he could always be seen walking around naked. He went on to explain that Haiti had no institution for the mentally unstable so they made their home among the masses. He followed it up with "you should see the woman that runs around in the same suit!"

My second week on the island brought more adventure than I was looking for. I was loading emergency medical supplies destined for a town called Hinche. It lay fifteen minutes on the other side of the mountain range smack dab in the middle of the valley. It was so tiny that I had already flown over it several times without ever knowing. I was supposed to drop my cargo in the care of the Red Cross. I had solicited as much information as I could from the missionary pilots that were familiar with the airstrip. The only words of caution that I received were "short runway." Armed with that, I overloaded the plane.

Reflecting back on my trip to the Arctic, I continued to load well beyond the max gross takeoff weight. I had already seen how much this plane could carry regardless of what the book said, and in my favor, I had ten thousand feet of runway. There was no doubt in my mind that it would fly flawlessly. When it looked like it couldn't hold anymore, I threw one more box inside and latched the door. I climbed into the pilot seat through the small crew door-window.

After I received clearance to depart, I made the standard left hand turn up and over the mountain range. I ducked between the clouds and the mountaintops and as soon as I was over the crest, I nosed the aircraft down and shadowed the terrain at two thousand feet. I checked the moving map display on the instrument panel. The field lay directly ahead. The dirt strip was coming into view. From my current distance, the runway looked sidewalk thin. I planned a low fly by to assess the field as well as warn any locals of my impending landing. As I closed in, the strip didn't appear to get any bigger. It still resembled a sidewalk and was just as they had said; very short. I descended to five hundred feet and lined myself up with the runway roughly five miles out. The treetops extended into the sky at the approach end, which meant that I would have to drop it onto the runway instead of a standard gradual descent. I could see the end of the tree line just before the runway and I made my final descent to one hundred feet above them. I slowed the plane and buzzed over the field. At the same time I passed over the approach end, I looked at my watch. I was going to calculate the runway length.

The townspeople below scattered in all directions pulling their livestock and corralling their chickens off of the common trail part time runway. The strip had walking paths worn across it from left to right and it was located in the center of town with houses on one side, trees to the other and concrete walls on both ends. The perimeter around it gave me the impression that this was the town square.

Imagine landing an airplane in the playground behind your house.

I pulled up at the far end and began my calculations. I figured about two thousand two hundred feet. I knew I could land it even though I was overweight, but there was no way I would be able to take off in the same configuration. I banked to the left to circle for the landing. The runway was clear from what I could see. Those down below knew I was coming in. When I returned to the five mile final approach mark, I had the plane slowed to its final speed and I was descending to treetop level. I dropped the gear and undoubtedly heard the scraping of the branches against the tires. I was right where I needed to be to tuck it into the short strip. As soon as I cleared the trees, I dropped the plane just inside of the concrete wall. As I began to brake, I saw from my left side that a goat had somehow escaped the grasp of its owner and ran out in front of me. I pulled back on the controls and to my surprise the plane leapt into the air high enough to clear the goat, but came back down hard on the dirt surface. I breathed a sigh of relief as the plane came to a stop. I put my head down in an effort to digest what had just happened. As I shook it off, I sat back then leaned over to unlatch my door. At that moment, thirty armed rebels dressed in camouflage with rifles in hand stepped out from under the cover of the trees. They wanted to talk to me.

I had no idea how I was going to bargain my way out of this. The Marine Corps had never taught me negotiating techniques unless the negotiations involved a rifle. I was reluctant to open the door, but I figured if I didn't, they would. The townspeople had gathered behind the rebels. I could hear the whispers of the native tongue, but couldn't understand a word. I figured at this point they would either shoot me outright or take my cargo and send me on my way. The children peeked through and around the adults standing in the shade line of the trees. It was customary for pilots to give the kids candy upon landing. Granted I had bags of candy on board, but at this point my safety took precedence over their joy.

The rebels talked amongst themselves until finally one of them approached and motioned for me to open the cargo door. I opened the door for his inspection. He looked over the boxes and turned back to rejoin his group. I looked around at the faces of everyone in my immediate area. Tension was in the air, but the faces weren't angry or hostile. The children continued to seek approval to approach the plane in search of the Candy Man's treasures. I hopped up on the wing and reached inside the crew door. I grabbed the candy and turned towards the children. The mob was like puppies trying to steal treats from a hand. I finally tore the bag open and tossed the candy in their direction.

When the children dispersed, the representative from the Red Cross arrived. The rebels turned their rifle sights in her direction. She showed no fear as she approached the man who had distinguished himself as the leader. I watched her as she walked into the rebel circle. The jibber-jabber sounds of French drifted in my direction. The mood was still apprehensive, but I was under the impression that the discussions between the two were evenly keeled.

The kids continued to beg for more candy as I crouched beneath the wing to escape the heat. I proceeded to monitor the progress of the negotiations. The townspeople were milling about and I had a hard time ascertaining whose side they were taking: the rebels or the lady from the Red Cross. She finally turned in my direction and approached. The formality of an introduction was completely disregarded, as both of us knew full and well that such a thing was irrelevant given the situation at hand.

"Good or bad?" I asked.

"We're ok," she assured me. "They'll help you unload the cargo."

With that, I stepped into the aircraft and began tossing boxes to the men outside the plane.

Twenty minutes later, I was roaring down the runway amid the smiles and waves from the children that I had showered with candy. They ran next to the plane like a puppy chasing a child as the school bus drives away.

I didn't experience anything like that again during my stay in Haiti, but the encounter made me apprehensive when I arrived at other unfamiliar fields. I remember landing in Mole St. Nicholas and I was on edge. It was my first flight after the trip into Hinche and I didn't know what to expect.

The town lay on the banks of a small bay on the northwest point of the island. Old wooden boats studded the beach. The ocean was picture perfect blue and the tropical breeze gave birth to small waves that waltzed across the inlet. The inlet carried upon its back a fishing boat loaded with fisherman. I stood on the embankment a hundred feet above them peering over the edge. When I was spotted, I found myself showered with greetings. No rifles, no hostile stares just the civility of friendly waves.

I actually found that the longer I remained the fonder I became. I had the pleasure of visiting many cities in Haiti and found myself wondering why the country was still considered to be third world. Cape Haitien was a city that at one time offered itself as a destination for many cruise ships, but the constant uncertainty and increasing crime discouraged tourists. The one thing that keeps Haiti from escaping poverty is Haiti itself. The country has resources and could capitalize tremendously on Caribbean tourism, but lack of infrastructure and a viable know-how has crippled its ability to do so.

I found Cape Haitien to be exactly the kind of city that I thrive in. It afforded the opportunity to mingle in the open markets and browse the shops of the locals. On one street, I could feel the vulnerability of being far from home and on the next, I found myself admiring the French architecture. Cars were racing up and down the roads head to head with horns blowing. The heart of this city was vibrant.

I sat at a tiny table under an immense concrete overhang at the Hotel Mont Joli. My waiter poured a Coca Cola in one of those ridiculously tall slender glasses with a toothpick umbrella jutting out of the top canted to one side. The food was the best I had had in Haiti.

After my lunch, I had a conversation with a nineteen-year old kid who had left the states in search of adventure. He was currently operating an orphanage where the oldest child was two years old. I was completely captivated and secretly jealous. Imagine the courage it took for him to pick up his life and move for more adventurous surroundings. That's life. Money can't buy what he was experiencing. He told me of the problems that he faced on a daily basis. No car, sporadic electricity, and worst of all, no funds to support the everyday needs of the orphans. Nineteen years old and he was tackling problems bigger than most of us will ever experience in our lives. It put my problems into perspective.

Cape Haitien was well aware of the coup that was sweeping the country. Canadian troops were in the midst of delivering a barrage of supplies to help with the recovery efforts. The rebels had destroyed the airport. The control tower had been ransacked and the radar was knocked out of service. The passenger terminal looked like it had been hit by a hurricane. The runway itself had gone unmolested, but the runway had issues long before the rebels stormed through. It was plenty long reaching up to eight thousand feet, but only four thousand was usable. The first half was solid concrete with the second half being blacktop, and where they met in the middle, engineering had experienced something truly baffling because the blacktop was two feet lower than the concrete. It literally put a wall at the halfway point. This meant that only the second half was useable. The local farmers used the first half as a bike path and they routinely herded their cattle across it.

Our chauffer DeVaulier turned out to be more than just the guy who drove me to work. He was a wonderful tour guide and I felt very secure traveling with him. He and I got on much better than I did with the other guys in the group. They were both religious whereas I am a non-believer so other than the job; we had no common thread between us.

DeVaulier and I, under any other set of circumstances, maybe in a different time and place, would have been hanging buddies. He often took me on out-of-the-way routes on our daily drive so I could see more than the crowded city streets. On one such drive, while circumventing the traffic in Petionville, we came upon a dead body lying face down. It had been pushed off to the side of the road and lay face down in the dirt with one arm tucked under the torso partially jutting from the corpse's right side. The legs were together with the knees facing away from the road as if the body had originally been lying on its side. I had seen bodies in the morgue before so this didn't shock me, but it did arouse compassion. Where was his family? Did anyone know? DeVaulier told me that the body had been there for a few days. A few days! People on the opposing side of the street continued with their everyday life. As we drove by, I realized that death in this country, no matter how cold and merciless, was everyday life.

We pulled over on the main thoroughfare immediately after passing through Petionville. We shared Cokes and ate cheese and crackers from a local market. We discussed certain repairs that needed to be done on his vehicle and we watched intently as the ladies sashayed by, smiling and winking before disappearing into the masses. The language barrier between us caused a lot to be lost and much of what we tried to converse about went unrecognized. He asked me what New York was like and was it beautiful in Miami. I tried my best to convey the message that he wanted to hear, but all said and done, it amounted to nothing more than head bobs and smiles. It would suffice for the moment.

When the time came to depart from the torn land of Haiti, I was more than ready. I needed a new set of surroundings where the job was concerned. I would have loved to stay as an adventurer, but that wouldn't pay the bills.

I knew that this assignment wasn't going to do much for my pay since I only got paid when I flew. Most of the flying in Haiti was twenty-five minutes here and fifteen minutes there, I didn't earn much for the duration of my stay. When it was all said and done, I averaged less than ten dollars an hour. It was an insult considering the hazardous conditions that I had been subjected to.

When I returned to Virginia, I walked into the offices of upper management.

"Where are the extra funds that I was told I was going to get?" I demanded.

"We were under the impression that everything was ok down there!" he replied.

"Ok?" I asked. "They've got bodies in the street, burning vehicles, shootings outside of our house, and I had rebel rifles in my face!" I cried. "Does that sound like everything was ok to you?"

"We weren't aware of any of this," came the lame duck reply.

"What?" I asked. "I've been talking to the project manager the whole time. He's well aware of what's going on down there."

"I'll look into it, but I can't make any promises," he said.

"Don't bother," I replied. "Here's my two week notice." And with that, I walked out the door. I was tired of being used and lied to. I had been lied to since the day I enlisted in the Marine Corps. I called Pete.

"So tell me about this jet job."

CHAPTER 23

Hitting Bottom

Pete had come through with the job that would be my introduction into the world of jets. It was the last, and much needed, addition to my résumé. It was the silver lining or so it would seem, but it didn't come without a price. Though it offered me a chance to aspire to new heights, it knocked me down a few rungs on the financial ladder saddling me with yet another pay cut. I was struggling to get by on twenty five thousand dollars a year. The American public seems to think that pilots make an atrocious amount of money. Quite the contrary. We live the same as everyone else, paycheck to paycheck, and even more so when we are trying to climb the ranks at the start of our careers.

I was going to have to get by on the small salary. The industry wasn't hiring, but with jet time under my belt I could assure myself that when the doors of aviation opened up again I would be a sought after candidate. I had to take this job or find another career. I had invested way too much to turn back now.

The job required that I relocate once again, this time to Roanoke, Virginia. I was looking forward to the new surroundings, but I wasn't looking forward to the move. I was fed up with the gypsy life that I had been living and longed for the stability of a home to go to at the end of the day. I still believed this world held a cookie cutter life for me with the big house, white picket fence and two-car garage. By the end of the month, my way of thinking would change drastically.

It was March of 2004 when I left the company near Harrisonburg for what seemed like greener pastures in Roanoke. My school for the new job didn't start until May, but the lease on my apartment was up. If I wanted to stay there on a month-to-month basis, it would increase my rent by three hundred dollars a month. I couldn't afford it. I was caught between a rock and a hard place.

Even if I had moved to Roanoke then, I wouldn't be able to afford an apartment on my own. I had made an arrangement with two other pilots that were employed with my new employer as well. We were going to share an apartment, but neither would be moving to Roanoke until May so I was forced to make a life changing decision; stay in a hotel or live in my truck. Though the new company had already put me on salary, it was hardly enough to pay my bills and afford a hotel for that length of time. Even the worst hotel in Harrisonburg cost over fifty dollars a night. I stayed there for three days before I realized there was no way I would be able to do it for the long term, not only because it would get expensive, but the tenants were a little off-putting as well. Most of them were drunks and drug addicts that constantly hung out under the stoop outside the rooms drinking and laughing until the wee hours of the morning. I figured if I stayed there, I would be in jail by the end of the week for beating someone. My life situation had me completely frazzled. I was a bomb ready to explode.

I elected to change my address to 1993 Ford Ranger pickup truck and decided to remain in Harrisonburg versus moving to Roanoke for the mere reason of familiarity with my surroundings. If I was going to be homeless, I wanted to at least be in a place where I felt safe. My worldly possessions, what little I had, were stored in a local storage facility so I had a place to keep things. I kept my suitcase on the floor of the truck and any extra clothes I had I put them on the seat next to me.

Most people can't fathom going from living in an apartment to living in a car and certainly not overnight. I broke it down to one simple question and that was, what do I need to survive? Food, clothing, and something to keep my head out of the rain; seemed simple enough. In my mind, it was a temporary sacrifice on the way to achieving my goal.

I tried to make my new home as comfortable as possible, but no matter what I did, I couldn't overcome the fact that the truck's cab was three feet by four feet. On the bright side, I was thankful for two things; One was that it was spring, which meant that it wasn't too hot during the day and not too cold at night, and two was the fact that I am short, which enabled me to curl up on the seat and close both doors when it came time to sleep. A plus if you want to lock the doors and increase your safety. I carried two day's supply of groceries in the cab at any one time and I routinely ate breakfast, lunch and dinner in the park that was located directly behind the apartment that I had previously rented. I ate the same things everyday: canned foods and fruit. It was cheap and required no preparation. I bathed by washing up at the sink in the park restroom usually very early or very late and often times I would use the facilities at the laundry mat or the rest stop on the interstate.

My situation, rather than discouraging me, allowed me the opportunity to really assess my life not just from the standpoint of "I'm homeless and broke," but more along the lines of my interest in material things. I no longer craved the American dream. I was living for whatever was in store for me around the next corner. I suddenly looked at houses as objects to hold worldly possessions and nothing more and I was already accomplishing that with a ten by ten storage facility so what was the point? I wasn't interested in money or fancy cars. I was interested in life and living for the moment. I no longer asked myself, "where will I be in five years?" I was asking myself, "where will I be next week?" Sure there were times when I felt humiliated and ashamed and there were times when I sat down and felt sorry for myself. But in the midst of my crumbled up and beaten down world, I still had a plan and I still had a goal.

I had gambled everything I had in life on a career that so far was a losing bet. Had September 11th, 2001 never happened, I would be very close to seeking employment with a major airline and well on my way to the life that my crystal ball had envisioned. It would have been so easy for me to throw in the towel and accept my circumstances. I was at rock bottom making snow angels out of dirt. I was better off when I was peddling drugs. No place to go and no place to be was taking its toll on me and it was only week three.

I lay awake at night thinking of what it would take to right my world. Money was what would pay off the insurmountable bill that aviation had created, but I was thinking further down the line. I couldn't remember a time when I didn't have debts to pay. What would life be like when I was finally able to straighten it out? I fell asleep listening to the rain pitter-patter on the metal roof of my truck. The rest of the world was tucking children into bed and saying prayers to a god that I was convinced didn't exist.

At the crack of dawn, I drove to the park and began the day with a bath in the sink and breakfast. I sat on a bench to watch the people who went by. In an instant, I was transformed into the Bench Man.

I could pick out the rich college kids versus those that came from more humble beginnings. I even spotted other homeless folks. I analyzed them, trying to sort the differences between them and me. I wondered if people could look at me and tell that I was on the street. It was hard to hold my head up at times even though I knew it was only a temporary situation.

I found myself spending my evenings watching little league baseball. It helped pass the time, but more importantly it warded off the feeling of loneliness that this lifestyle was harboring. All my friends in Virginia lived in the northern part of the state. I would have gladly driven the two and a half hours to see them, but I just didn't have the money to make the trip. I didn't have friends in Harrisonburg. Most of the guys I knew from the job that I had just left were pilots that spent lots of time on the road. I continued to keep up the façade with the folks back home. "I'm doing great. I'm really looking forward to this new job!" I would tell them. I didn't want anyone to know the truth. I remember talking to my best friend Jeff from my truck while I was sitting in a rest stop. I couldn't even tell him that my life was in the toilet. I didn't want to admit that my quest to become a pilot was a bad idea. He made his life sound like it was the greatest thing on earth. I was so jealous, but at the same time so happy for him. Just hearing him talk pushed me within one step of turning with my tail tucked between my legs and running back to Iowa to settle on that end-of-the-line factory job. I was ready to admit to my family and friends that I had failed in life. It seemed like flying had beaten me the same way bodybuilding had. I was a few days from attending jet school.

Being homeless for six weeks not only changed the way I viewed life, but also nearly crushed my desire to fly. I now understood why people settled for jobs and careers that they really didn't want to be in. I saw how easy it would be to situate myself in a lamentable job and miserably wait for retirement. They did it for stability. They did it because they were afraid to live the way I was living. I could see myself ending up like the masses, living my life for two days at the end of the week. It was a horrible thought, but being homeless almost made it reality.

By the time I arrived for my first day of jet school, I was filled with doubt that this was even the right path for me to travel. I knew I could pass this thing with flying colors if I just applied myself. That first jet for any pilot is a bit unnerving to say the least. The information was fed to me with a fire hose and emphasized with a "get it or get out" attitude. I spent eight hours a day in class and another three or four at night studying. The bookwork was only half of the learning process. The other half consisted of what had been my nemesis from my inception into pilot training: the simulator! I was completely overwhelmed. I had been flying a plane with instruments that were considered old technology and now I was thrust into the seat of what was considered state of the art with computers and glass screens. I struggled with it and even opted for an extra day of simulator practice before the test. To make matters worse, the guy who was tasked with testing me was a real piece of work. I had never met someone so disgruntled. It was evident that he was harboring resentment towards the industry and he wasn't here because he wanted to be. He didn't give me anything that I couldn't handle, but I let him intimidate me completely, so much so, that I failed the check ride.

That was it for me. I now had the excuse I needed to go find that misery that started on Monday and ended on Friday. I had failed at the second career that I had chosen. Bodybuilding had left me a shelf full of trophies and pictures safely tucked away in boxes. Aviation was only going to leave me with a credit card statement that would haunt me for years to come.

I was scheduled to re-take the simulator check ride a week later. In the interim, I flew back to Virginia with my head hanging. I didn't need this misery. I could make twenty five thousand dollars anywhere without the hassles that contaminated the aviation world. The police departments that I had once turned down were looking like a good idea. The company reassured me with positive pep talks. I didn't have the courage to tell them that I was on the verge of walking away. I kept that to myself and used the next week for a bit of soul searching.

I'm not sure why I even went back to Virginia since I didn't have a home to go to, but again familiarity helped me solidify that decision. I dug out a credit card that I had tucked away in storage and pointed the truck towards northern Virginia. I returned to the old haunts that I used to frequent. I went back to the restaurants to see who was still around.

Some faces I recognized; others were new. That was a sign that many of the people that had been such a wonderful part of my life a few short years before, were now out there in the real world facing their own trials the same as me. I needed to leave my current world behind for the carefree world that I once lived in.

I left the restaurant at about 1:00 a.m. and drove to the neighborhood where Elwood Scott and I had shared so many conversations. I thought about how close he and I had been to reaching our goals in professional sports. I thought about those nights sitting on the steps sharing our two-cents as to what we thought was out there beyond the stars. I remembered his voice and his stories. It was enough to fill me with laughter at a time when I shouldn't have been laughing.

So, I charged a few hundred dollars on top of the debt I already owed. I didn't care. That drive to northern Virginia ended with laughter and it let me escape back to a time when life wasn't kicking me. It rekindled my fire for the decision to leave the wretched midnight shift for a better life. All the goals and reasons reintroduced themselves to me as I drove back to Harrisonburg in the wee hours of the morning. I hadn't lost sight of them; they were simply buried underneath my self-pity.

I paid for my own ticket back to Dallas and the hotel and rental car as well. It was only more debt on a plastic card. I could care less. This job was never going to pay it off anyway; this job was never meant to be the one to take me to retirement. Somehow I lost sight of that fact, but once I accepted the understanding that this job was simply for jet experience, a weight was lifted. I knew I couldn't pay off the debt and concentrate on flying and focus on my housing situation or lack thereof all at once. I passed the second chance check ride refocused and rejuvenated and put the episode behind me.

CHAPTER 24

Roanoke

I finally relocated to Roanoke and moved into an apartment with two other pilots. The rent was a little over four hundred a month, which split three ways was very doable even on the low salary that I was making. I took with me enough belongings to be comfortable, but left most of my things in storage. It was a typical airline crash pad. It was cheap and that was the only qualifying factor it needed to satisfy us. The accommodations were adequate. The kitchen was deathly small and the carpet worn and stained. It was configured for two bedrooms, but we used the den as a third. The other two pilots rotated a week on, a week off so there was seldom a time when all three of us were there at the same time. That was good since there was only one bathroom. One guy slept on an air mattress and the other slept on a spring mattress thrown directly onto the floor. We had the bare minimums that entitled us to call the place furnished.

The money aside, I enjoyed Roanoke. I became good friends with the guys that I roomed with. We frequented the clubs in town and became friends with our neighbors. I even bought a piece of home gym equipment and began working out again. I needed to lose a few pounds so I cleaned up my diet and began running a few miles every couple of days. My work schedule was perfect. I worked eight days then had six off. That gave me plenty of time to hold down a part time mechanic job at Eagle's Nest Airport about an hour to the north. The extra money was exactly what I needed to start digging my way out of the financial hole that I was still in.

The new job was a startup company. We flew strictly air ambulance flights so the flying was sporadic. As soon as I started to get in the groove and really learn the airplane, then we wouldn't fly for two weeks. It was frustrating.

My friend Pete was at the helm as the Director of Operations and my roommate Ramiro was the Chief Pilot, which made both of them my bosses. Pete was in charge of the day-to-day operations and Ramiro was in charge of everything that pertained to the pilot corps. I can't think of a better guy to have taught me how to fly a jet than Ramiro. His patience with fledgling pilots made him a born teacher. There are so many captains in this industry that don't have a clue how to teach a young aspiring co-pilot how to achieve the next level of flying skills. They harbor the pathetic training techniques from the '70s and have a tendency to verbally abuse and belittle. Co-pilots will make mistakes, there's no doubt about that, but as a captain you have to be able to help them learn from those mistakes. If you can't do that, then you're a failure at being a captain and should probably be looking for work in another field. If captains were promoted on merit versus seniority, the airline industry would benefit tremendously. The captain is, first and foremost, a teacher and a button pusher second. Ramiro was an extraordinary teacher.

The home life in Roanoke began to feel normal. I was spending most of my off time working at Eagle's Nest Airport, and was slowly working my way out of debt, which was now teetering around twenty thousand dollars. I lost that fifteen pounds of extra weight that I had been carrying and finally got my body back in shape. I also made frequent trips to Northern Virginia to maintain friendships and stroll down memory lane. There's nothing wrong with going back, just don't lose sight of what's out front. Roanoke was fast becoming a place that I would have fond memories of.

The more we flew the more my skills improved. I was really enjoying the life of a pilot on the go. My other roommate, Robert, and I took up tennis and going to the park in an effort to stay out of the apartment. His nickname was Pizzaman. He had a long drawn out last name that had Italian roots, but no one ever pronounced it correctly. The first part of it sounded like "pizza" hence the name.

Pizzaman and I were scheduled to make a flight to Brazil to pick up an American patient who was in bad shape after a botched operation. The flight time down there was scheduled for ten hours with four fuel stops. Our jet just didn't have the long range that some others do. We would first stop in the Bahamas, then Venezuela, and clear Brazilian customs in Manaus. We would then continue on to Brasilia, Brazil and finally to Belo Horizonte, which was located a few hours northwest of Rio de Janerio.

We arrived in Belo Horizonte absolutely exhausted. The medical personnel traveling with us went directly to the hospital to get the status on the patient's condition. Pizzaman and I went to the hotel. The plan was to launch the flight back to the states the next day in the early afternoon. When the time came to load up and go, we got our first look at the passenger-patient. He was in bad shape, so much so, that right after he was loaded on the plane, he flat-lined. The doctors on the scene were able to revive and stabilize him, but I was having doubts as to the successful outcome of the flight.

After a forty-five minute delay, we set out with our now stabilized passenger and headed to the capital city of Brasilia. About midway through the flight, the flight nurse poked her head into the cockpit and informed us that the patient was using more oxygen than what the medical personnel in Belo Horizonte had told us. We were told he was using forty percent when in fact he was being kept alive using roughly eighty percent. We didn't have a bottle big enough to sustain this amount of usage. Pizzaman was faced with the decision to turn back or continue to Brasilia and reassess our situation. After a discussion with the flight nurse, he opted to press on.

We figured that we could refill the oxygen bottle at every fuel stop, but after landing in Brasilia and researching the plan further we found out that we wouldn't be able to refill in Caracas, Venezuela. Now we were faced with the decision to return the patient to the hospital in Belo Horizonte. We couldn't afford to go on with the flight and not be able to sustain life for the patient. If he died on the plane in another country, it would become an international incident. We would be held wherever we landed until the red tape was cleared. That could possibly keep us in a foreign country for weeks. Pizzaman made the right call when he decided to return to Belo Horizonte.

Meanwhile, with all the decision making being done, the patient was using up what little oxygen was left in our big bottle. The flight nurse had three small hand bottles that she was prepared to use to sustain him. I called the Brazilian maintenance personnel to refill our bottle. They had the ability to refill us, but their bottle fittings didn't match ours. The flight nurse began using hand bottle number one. We were now faced with the decision of putting the patient in the hospital in Brasilia, but just as we were about to do that, one of the mechanics said he could make a fitting back in his shop and return within fifteen minutes. Robert and I looked at each other in disbelief. It was a gamble, but Pizzaman agreed to it. The mechanic sped away. The flight nurse started the patient on hand bottle number two. The patient was now bloating and his skin was purple and green. He was in dire shape.

The mechanic returned with a proper fitting. By the time we managed to refill the big oxygen bottle, the flight nurse was halfway finished with the third and final hand held bottle. We had come very close to losing the patient and certainly would have had it not been for the mechanic. We loaded the plane and returned to Belo Horizonte. The patient was put in an ambulance headed back to the hospital, but died before they made it there. The whole day had been a morbid experience. I reflected on how lucky we are in this country to have the medical facilities that we have. The entire crew was somber even though we made all the right decisions. We checked back into the hotel and agreed to meet at the hotel bar to try to forget the day's events.

The air ambulance job lasted almost a year. Pete left to raise horses and Ramiro bolted for a job in Denver. I followed suit by taking up employment in North Carolina. Pizzaman was the last to leave the apartment in Roanoke.

CHAPTER 25

North Carolina

I accepted employment with Segrave Aviation, which required me to relocate once again, this time to Hickory, North Carolina. I didn't have a problem with that since it was only a little more than three hours to the south of Roanoke. More importantly, it was a pay raise. Hickory's cost of living was very low compared to anything in Virginia. I found a beautiful two-bedroom apartment in a very nice section of town. The rent was only four hundred dollars a month. Things were finally falling into place.

The job was simple. We flew the aircraft owner half of the month, then the plane was chartered the other half. That's how it's normally done in the charter world. A person who owns a jet will hire a management company to take care of everything that has to do with the aircraft. Setting up charters to help with the cost of ownership and keeping track of aircraft maintenance are two of the most prominent benefits a management company can offer. They obviously charge a fee for this service, but at the same time they obtain the use of the airplane without having to pay the expense of owning one.

Though a nice place to live, Hickory itself was definitely not a place that I was ever going to call home. I lived in a quiet neighborhood on the northwest side of town at the end of a cul de sac. The apartment was located directly on the final approach corridor into the Hickory Regional Airport. I enjoyed being close to work. The town had everything I needed to survive. So why wouldn't I call it home? First and foremost was the fact that I was never going to be converted into thinking that NASCAR was actually an exciting sport. I fly a jet that travels at five hundred miles per hour. Rest assured a car going in circles at one hundred and eighty is not something that gets my adrenaline flowing. Secondly, the government of the town of Hickory, specifically the traffic management division, was slower than the second coming of Jesus.

Growing up in Iowa, I was accustomed to avenues running in one direction and streets in the other. Living in the Washington D.C. area, I became acclimated to the use of the alphabet and names to distinguish streets. Most of the United States uses one of those methods or a variant of to help their inhabitants navigate to and from within the city limits. Hickory, North Carolina on the other hand wasn't able to comprehend such simplicity and logic. I lived on fourteenth Avenue NW, not to be confused with Fourteenth Avenue NW Place, Fourteenth Avenue NW Street, or Fourteenth Avenue Place, all of which existed.

The best thing about Hickory other than the road leading out of town was the minor league baseball team. I spent a lot of my off time at the ballpark. It was just nice to get away and relax and was basically the only form of entertainment Hickory had to offer.

There were two other pilots based in Hickory. One of them was about my age and we hit it off immediately. His name was Todd. I identified with him even more so after I had heard his story of how he came to be in aviation. Here was a guy who had graduated college in Illinois, packed up his car and headed to California with half a plan in place. He slept in his car on the beach until he found a flight instructor job. He was bound and determined to make things work. He was another casualty of September 11th and corporate merging, but to talk to him, you would never have guessed it. The first thing he said to me was, "Ramiro made you a good pilot, but I'm going to make you a great one!" He was a great teacher. I've never had so much fun as a pilot as when I flew with Todd.

The other pilot, Charlie, was a retired Air National Guard pilot. He had also spent time flying with the airlines. He used to joke that if an airline wanted to go out of business all they needed to do was hire him. Most of the ones he had flown for were no longer in operation.

One night Charlie and I had flown to our destination and opted to grab some pizza and retire to our rooms. Along with the pizza, Charlie decided to grab a quart bottle of beer. As we drove to the hotel in our rental car, we made a few wrong turns, which flustered poor Charlie. He was ready for his pizza and beer. In his haste to get us to our hotel, he ran a red light and decided to stop midway through it. He hammered the brakes and his pizza rolled off the front seat and landed out of the box under his feet! I did everything I could to not laugh. He spewed out a graceful display of obscenities, threw the pizza back in its box and continued the drive. Within ten minutes, we were at our destination. I told Charlie that I would meet him inside after I parked the car. I was trying my best to help calm him down.

I met him in the hotel lobby a few minutes later and found him pacing back and forth, his face a deep, deep angry red.

"What's the matter now?" I asked.

"Well," he started, trying to catch his breath. "I put my beer in my garment bag and my luggage fell over and busted the thing all over my clothes!" he confessed. He mumbled another beautiful stream of colorful words as he toted his dirt-covered pizza and beer soaked clothes off to his room.

I laughed till I cried and called Todd immediately to share the fun. Charlie was a great sport when it came to laughing at himself. In fact, the next morning he was the one to state that he enjoyed the pizza and managed to wring enough beer from his clothes to wet his taste buds!

I was very content flying for Segrave. I wasn't going to get rich, but I was well on my way to getting out of debt and was actually saving money.

I kept in touch with Ramiro after we parted ways and I received an email from him saying that he was going back to Virginia to continue what he had started with the air ambulance company, which by this time, had changed its operation to a full time charter provider. It didn't take him long to convince me to return as well. I look back now and realize that that was a bad move, but I was chasing the almighty dollar in the hopes of clearing my debts once and for all. Ramiro had made me an offer that was impossible for me to turn down given my current financial situation.

That left me with an issue of a training contract with Segrave. I had signed a contract specifically stating that if they paid for my training, I would give them one full year of employment. I was three months shy of fulfilling my end of the deal. This is nothing new in aviation and when a contract is breeched in this manner; the difference is normally pro-rated and paid off or completely forgotten about. The pro-rated amount left on my contract was roughly two thousand dollars, but they were going to hold me to the full amount or at least a higher negotiated sum, which in the end turned out to be six thousand dollars. I added the six grand to what I already owed. I once again packed it up and moved back to Virginia. Ramiro had already begun to lay down roots and was leasing a house in a beautiful sub-division of Waynesboro. Once again we became roommates as I accepted his offer to sublet his basement apartment.

The company's planes were flying nonstop. I spent ten to fifteen days on the road at a time. Even though my role had changed, the problems in the head office remained the same as before. The CEO still hadn't figured out how to successfully manage the company. His lack of knowledge in the charter business crippled us. On top of that, he had a volatile temper so when something didn't go as planned; he would explode in a barrage of obscenities at anyone in his path. He had fired so many people that the FAA was now keeping a close eye on our operation. Whenever a charter company sustains a number of management changes in a short period of time, it's considered to be unstable. This made us more susceptible to FAA audits and closer oversight. It's the same with the airlines when they file bankruptcy. The FAA knows that they are going to try to cut costs and one of the first things an airline will do is try to skimp on its maintenance, so the FAA will step up its inspection of that maintenance operation.

This constant scrutiny coupled with the CEO's managerial ineptitude hampered the company's ability to grow and move forward. We still hadn't captured a solid customer base and he had once again cut his own throat by signing an exclusive contract with another agency that allowed them to use our planes eighty percent of the time. Even if we had begun to reign in customers of our own, we didn't have the ability to use our own planes to charter them.

The CEO blamed the employees for everything that wasn't right within the company. He fired the Chief Pilot and basically made me an offer that I couldn't refuse. Become the Chief Pilot or I'll shut the doors. He also coaxed Pete to come back and try to save the sinking ship, but two days after my appointment, he closed up shop. Pete and I were never given a chance to rectify things.

The real reasons finally began to surface as to why he decided to pull the plug. His family was very wealthy. His parents still gave him a monthly allowance rumored to be eighty five thousand dollars a month. He had never worked a day in his life. This was just a project for him. He didn't care whether it was successful or not. In the months leading up to the shut down, it was rumored that he received twelve million dollars as part of an early inheritance. It was the excuse he needed to walk away. When we asked him what he was going to do now that we were out of business, he leaned back in his chair and said, "Well, I'm blessed and I don't have to work for a living so I'm going to go back to enjoying life." He didn't care about the lives he had just ruined. The day we got our notices, he was on the phone purchasing a luxury motor home so he could take his family out to see the country. He was planning a vacation while the rest of us were wondering where our lives were headed.

CHAPTER 26

Triumph

We remained on the payroll for one month after we received our notices. It was pure luck that during this time I landed a new job. Though it was a start up operation, it was a risk I had to take. I was too close to being out of debt. By now, the airlines were hiring again and I was applying, but those jobs take time to materialize. I needed this job until they called to say "Welcome Aboard!"

When I packed my things for the sixth time in five years, I was actually smiling. Oh I dreaded the move and everything it entailed, but I didn't fear what was out there waiting for me. I climbed up into the moving truck with everything in this world that I could call mine. I put Virginia in my rear view mirror. Twenty years and nothing to show for it. It was time to move on. I cranked up the radio and headed west. I had a new job and that's all I needed. I would figure out the rest later.

I made it as far as Las Vegas. It's only appropriate that a guy who gambled it all would find himself here. Las Vegas, I'm convinced it's Spanish for Bad Tattoo. Everyone here has at least one. It's not really a city at all. There's no Wall Street or Rush Street and there isn't a skyscraper downtown that isn't a hotel-casino. Take those away and you're left with concrete huts covered with red clay tiles. This is where I am hanging my hat for the time being.

When I first pulled into town, I had no place to live. For the first week, I made myself at home in that wonderful truck. I slept in the underground parking garages of the major casinos and cleaned up in the bathroom at the airplane hangar of my new employer. The Vegas heat was brutal and the air conditioner in my truck didn't work. I didn't have to live like this. I could have afforded an apartment, but then I wouldn't be able to continue paying off my debt or saving for retirement. It was another sacrifice that I was willing to make. Eventually, I negotiated a cheap rate at a local hotel and began staying there when I was in town. Fortunately, the new job kept me on the go. I spent an average of only ten days per month in Las Vegas, which kept my monthly living expenses well below what it would have cost me to rent an apartment. A bed and a shower is all I needed and the hotel provided that. Every now and then, I still slept in my truck. Old habits die hard.

Again, I had my moments of self-pity. There were times when I broke down. I was flying passengers that had more money in their wallet than I had in the bank. I tried not to think about it and concentrated my thoughts and efforts towards landing that airline job that was just around the corner.

I spent a lot of my time walking the Vegas strip and wandering in the local parks. Las Vegas could rival Washington D.C. with the number of homeless people that live within its limits. Technically, I was homeless, but I knew that I was far above the situations that the local homeless people were in. I had the drive and determination to achieve the goal I had set years before. As I looked around at the park benches, I could tell that these folks had already thrown in the towel. I held my head high because I knew that I had come so close to joining them, but through perseverance and sheer will I came out on top. I was never afraid to live in a car. I was never afraid to sacrifice everything for the happiness that I desired. Yes doing those two things made me a changed person. I'm hoping that the changes were for the better. I'm not afraid to sit and talk to that guy on the bench in the hopes of sparking something inside of him that will drive him to better his situation. It tears me apart to see people who are living this way.

I accept the blame for the hard road that my path to success followed. Some things were out of my control, but I made some bad decisions along the way. However, I've always been one to overcome and adapt subscribing to the theory that I got myself into this mess and I'll get myself out. I still hold on to the belief that you should never settle for anything and you should never let "No" be the final answer. You have one shot at life. If you're not happy with what life gives you, change it. Set a goal and go after it with everything you've got.

I split my time between a hotel and my truck for over a year. My journey was a difficult one, but I'm a different person because of it. Today, I'm soaring the skies at thirty seven thousand feet and five hundred miles per hour just as I had planned and I often look out the cockpit window and reflect on what it took to get here. What would I change? Not a thing. Because I had to climb over the hurdles that I did, I learned valuable lessons and because of that, I consider myself absolutely rich with wisdom. It may sound strange when I say that the climb getting here was more exciting than being here, but I somehow feel that my life is a bit on the dull side now. Things are more predictable and I'm living for what's five years down the road, not just for what's around the corner.

Today, I have financially recovered. I'm currently looking to buy property and build a house and though I will always have a special place in my heart for that 1993 Ford pickup, I'm contemplating buying a new vehicle. I'm even planning a vacation. It will be the first in nine years. Trust me when I say it's long overdue.

I don't know that my story has a moral to it; not an intended one anyway. I simply wanted to share it in the hopes of giving someone who may be in the same situation that I was a boost of confidence. I'm proof that life's difficulties can be overcome. Mountains are made for climbing. Don't be afraid of life and the challenges that it may present. Don't be afraid to live in your truck. Today, when the plane taxis in after the last flight of the day, I'm the guy who walks out of the cockpit smiling and like that pilot that changed the course of my life; I won't hesitate to tell you that I have the greatest job in the world.

Index

Bibliography

The Franklin Cover-Up Child Abuse, Satanism, and Murder in Nebraska. By John W. DeCamp.
Second Edition 1996 AWT, Inc.

George Bush: The Unauthorized Biography. By Webster G. Tarpley and Anton Chaitkin.
Executive Intelligence Review, January 1991

The Man Who Killed Boys: The John Wayne Gacy, Jr. Story. By Clifford L. Linedecker.
St. Martin Press, NY, NY 1980

Johnny Gosch, Jeff Gannon, Hunter Thompson, and the Unraveling of a Troubling Tale. By Tim Schmitt. Looking Glass News as posted on Lookingglassnews.org 09-03-06

The Johnny Gosch Foundation, Ted Gunderson Report 06-28-00

The Franklin Cover-Up Again. Independent Media Center. Interview with Noreen Gosch. By Charlene Fassa. 08-15-05

Mysteries of the Mind with Alex Merklinger. 4-part interview with Ted Gunderson and Jim Rothstein.

The Universal Seduction, Piercing the Veils of Deception website, via prisonplanet.com, excerpt from interview with Jim Rothstein.

Conspiracy of Silence, Video by the Discovery Channel and Yorkshire Television

Acknowledgments

I offer my sincere gratitude to American Book Publishing—the editors, designers and production staff.

Thank you to my family. To my brother and sister for your support and understanding. To my father for the friendship we now share. To my grandparents for always being there.

Billy 'white shoes' Johnson for the memory of Elwood; Harry Chaykum, Delaware County Times; Louis Avery and the Family of the great Elwood Scott; Carol Swenson, McPherson College; and Doc Brown for your words of encouragement and the friendship we share.

To Pete Twisdale for giving me doors of opportunity when no one else would. Ron Wehde for introducing me to Tolkien and a love for writing, and you didn't think I was listening!

To the great people of Iowa for being the best people on the planet and claiming me as one of your own and to all my wonderful friends in the sleepy little town of CAMANCHE, IOWA.

Special thanks to Courtney Fries.

In loving memory of Jeffrey Lee Fall

About the Author

B. Michael Fett is a former United States Marine who was once a two-time nationally qualified bodybuilder. He is currently a commercial pilot based in Denver, Colorado. He holds a Bachelor of Science Degree in Aviation Management and is also a licensed aircraft mechanic. Though he currently lives in Las Vegas, he calls home a small town in the great state of Iowa. He can be reached at bmichaelfett.com.